FOLLOW

→

"This book is moving, challenging, and inspiring. Katie Prejean McGrady always finds a way to get you nodding along with her and she is always authentic. While modern culture is often lacking in common sense, this book is a wonderful invitation back to sensible thought and prayer. We are lucky to have Katie as a teacher and will richly benefit from her wisdom here. *Follow* is a gift to all who want a relationship with Jesus but just don't know exactly where to start."

Mark Hart
Executive Vice President
Life Teen

"How does someone follow Jesus in our world today? Katie Prejean McGrady has given us a true gift—a practical, authentic, and intensely personal account of what it means to follow Jesus through prayer, scripture, service, sacraments, adoration, and evangelization. Katie takes your hand and leads you to Jesus. What a well-written, spot-on, and helpful book that is greatly needed for young Catholics finding their way today!"

Sarah Swafford
Author of *Emotional Virtue*

"*Follow* isn't just a book to read, it's a book to do. Katie Prejean McGrady is the Ms. Frizzle of Catholicism, walking teens through the most foundational ways that their Catholic faith invites them to take chances, avoid mistakes, and get messy in their pursuit of Christ. The book needs no prerequisites, offering an introduction to prayer, scripture, sacraments, and service that will both encourage and inspire a seasoned follower while not overwhelming new disciples."

Alison Blanchet
Youth and Campus Minister
St. John the Evangelist Catholic Church and School
Panama City, Florida

"Knowing and following Jesus is often confusing and frustrating, especially for youth. Katie Prejean McGrady combines theological substance, relevant personal witness, plenty of humor, insight, practical suggestions, and step-by-step sequences to help teens know, love, and serve Jesus. She has produced an accessible field manual for living as a Catholic teen today. This will be a book teens visit and revisit time and again, as a source of comfort, direction, and inspiration."

Roy Petitfils
Counselor, author, and speaker

"I would probably be the pope by now if someone had shared this book with me when I was a teen! Understanding who Jesus is may seem difficult and distant, but Katie Prejean McGrady provides a clear road map to Christ. *Follow* unpacks practices for a personal relationship with Jesus Christ in the very best ways for a twenty-first-century Christian. Whether your journey is just beginning or has been going on for years, Katie's stories and suggestions will lead you straight to Jesus."

Bill Staley
Director of Youth and Young Adult Ministry

Diocese of Nashville

"I absolutely loved Katie's book! *Follow* guides you to freely give your whole heart to God and how truly awesome it is to be in love with the Lord! Katie shows step by step how to encounter Jesus and spread his love to those around you."

Meredith O.
High school junior

"*Follow* is not a step-by-step instruction manual for how to encounter Jesus Christ. It is so much more. Katie's relatable stories make this book that much easier to love. Every teen truly looking to follow Christ should read *Follow*!"

Margaret B.
High school senior

"Whether you have just entered the faith or have been a believer for years, Katie's book serves as a 'how-to' guide for prayer, the Gospel, the sacraments, and reflecting Jesus through self-sacrifice and good acts. *Follow* outlines the essential steps it takes to embark on a lifelong journey. A journey not *for* Jesus but *with* him."

Samuel C.
High school junior

FOLLOW

YOUR LIFELONG ADVENTURE
WITH JESUS

Katie Prejean McGrady

Ave Maria Press AVE Notre Dame, Indiana

Founded in 1865, Ave Maria Press is a ministry of the United States Province of Holy Cross.

www.avemariapress.com

Paperback: ISBN-13 978-1-59471-823-6

E-book: ISBN-13 978-1-59471-824-3

Cover illustration by Samantha Watson.

Cover and text design by Samantha Watson.

Printed and bound in the United States of America.

Library of Congress Cataloging-in-Publication Data is available.

To my Tommy,
the best companion on the journey

To my Rosie,
whose adventure is just beginning

CONTENTS

PREFACE

In August 2016, I found myself in California on the UCLA campus for a gathering that brought together more than two thousand teens from across the Archdiocese of Los Angeles. It was my final event at the end of a long summer of traveling. Over the prior two months, I'd led service camps in Virginia, spoken at conferences in Toronto and Missouri, filmed a couple of shows at EWTN in Alabama, and spent a week at a summer camp in the wide-open cornfields of Iowa. It had been a fruitful, busy, exhausting few months on and off planes and in and out of hotel rooms. Los Angeles was my last stop, and I had just one keynote to go. Forty-five minutes with a few stories, some funny pictures, a couple of well-made theological points about striving for holiness and a relationship with Jesus, and then I was headed back to Louisiana to end my summer and begin my fifth year of teaching. Little did I know that those forty-five minutes in Los Angeles would completely change my ministry and my life.

The keynote went well: the crowd laughed when I hit the punch lines, they were moved during my more dramatic stories, and they nodded their heads when I made my key points. My measure of a talk is how still the audience sits. Granted, that may sometimes be an indicator that the group is bored and has fallen asleep, but more often stillness means that an audience is captivated and listening closely. The theater full of Californians was quite still that particular day.

Pleased with myself and proud of my work, I left the stage and headed toward the speaker hospitality room to grab a Diet Coke when a young man rounded the corner and marched right up to me.

"Hey! Can I talk to you?" he called out. I prepared myself for the usual posttalk chitchat and commentary, all the while thinking about how thirsty I was and how badly I wanted to sit down.

"Sure," I said, prepared to hear something like "You're so funny" or "Thanks for your honesty" or "I liked your stories."

"So, you were talking about Jesus up there."

Thinking he was being sarcastic, I dished the sarcasm right back. "Yeah . . . that's what I was talking about," I hastily said.

"Well, I just need to ask you, then: Who is Jesus? Like, really?" His voice was eager, curiosity covering his face.

Taken aback, I stood in shock for a moment. Wasn't this exactly what I had just given my entire forty-five-minute keynote about?

The young man quickly continued, "And how can I get to know him? Like, for myself? How can I get to know him for real?"

His question was so pure, so genuine, so honest, that I just stood there in complete confusion. I was positive I had just talked about those very topics for nearly an hour! The audience had been still; they seemed to be listening. Yet here stood this young man with genuine curiosity and what I could see was a heartfelt plea for answers to these two simple questions.

I stuttered out a quick answer, trying to briefly summarize what I'd just said on stage, but I could tell I wasn't satisfying him. I was being vague, speaking in generalities, making references to all the points I'd just made that had clearly prompted him to have these two questions in the first place.

As the awkwardness grew, and frustration with myself and my lack of articulate answers to what seemed like simple questions, we heard, "Hey, come on, man . . . it's time to go. It's our turn to eat dinner!"

Thank God for punctual chaperones, I thought to myself.

The young man nodded at the adult and turned back to me and said, "I just want to know who he is. No offense or nothing. Your talk was funny and all, I just don't think I know Jesus yet and you sounded like you do, so I was just wondering what I could do to get to know him too, ya know?"

As he walked away, I stood there in stunned silence. He did think my talk was funny after all. Apparently, that's all it had been for him.

That brief exchange was easily one of the most challenging conversations I've ever had with a teenager. His questions stopped me cold. I wasn't really offended that I had just spoken on the exact topic of his questions or that he hadn't heard what I thought I had just told him. I was disappointed in myself, thrown off by the fact that I clearly hadn't articulated things properly or given a straightforward message to help him on his own journey of faith. In the moment, I had been caught off guard, just stuttering through a shoddy synopsis of the very same talk he'd just heard me give.

In the aftermath, as I kept replaying the conversation over and over in my head, I became frustrated: Why did this kid come to me in the first place? I was just a speaker he'd only seen one time—just minutes before we spoke. Why was I to be trusted with the task of telling him how to get to know Jesus and encounter him in an authentic way? Didn't he have a youth minister? Didn't he have parents? My frustration quickly turned to fear. What if I had said the wrong thing when I did try to answer him? What if my incomplete, short answers weren't enough? What if all I had done was confuse this poor kid even more, making it harder for him to ever have a relationship with Jesus at all?

My encounter with this young man left me shaken. I was challenged as a teacher, writer, and Catholic speaker to come up with some sort of well-articulated, straightforward answers to what seemed like easy questions

But I couldn't. I froze. For some reason, I didn't have answers to those two fundamental questions on which so much of what I believe and do in life depend. I couldn't figure out why I didn't have answers, and that's when I grew angry. Why couldn't I just lay it out there, saying exactly who Jesus is and how I got to the point where I could say I knew him? How hard could it possibly be to just go through the step-by-step process of meeting and falling in love with the Savior of the World? Clearly I'd gone through those steps at some point (or at least this kid thought I had), so why was it so hard to just explain that now?

Over the next several weeks, I slowly came to accept that there isn't a simple way to uncover the identity of Christ Jesus. It's not just a one-and-done task: read a book, earn a badge, get the certificate, and wear the T-shirt that declares "I know Jesus." Getting to know Jesus is ultimately about setting out on a journey of biblical proportions. It's about meeting, coming to know, falling in love with, and growing an authentic relationship with this Middle Eastern carpenter-turned-rabbi who lived more than two thousand years ago. Following this man who changed everything, shaped the course of human history, and literally saved the world with what he said and did is a wonderful, crazy, beautiful adventure, and I want to help you experience precisely that.

That young man in Los Angeles asked questions to which I gave no satisfying answers, and that forced me to begin unpacking and rethinking everything I thought I already knew about Jesus. I couldn't ignore his queries and just walk away from his genuine curiosity. I needed to figure out, even if just for myself, exactly how someone meets Jesus and gets to know him in an authentic, life-altering way. How did I know Jesus beyond the textbooks in the classroom or the talks given from a stage? When did I meet him for myself? What did I do to meet him in the first place? I needed to be able to articulate all of that in such a way that it wasn't confusing, didn't come off as condescending, and wasn't just some rote repetition of everything else we've all heard before.

It wasn't until I began looking at my own life and started to really examine the watershed moments when I've encountered Jesus that I began to find those answers. I had to identify the times when I've seen Jesus, grown to know him personally, and experienced his infinite love. This process then led me to begin to identify and name the practical steps I'd taken to let him into my life in the first place and remain in relationship with him.

This book is about those moments—the days I've been filled with laughter and great joy, and also those when I was fraught with confusion and even moved to tears. These are the stories of events that have scared me straight and shaken me up. They're stories of sacrifice, patience, peace, excitement, insecurity, and assurance. These are moments when I've stood at the foot of the Cross, weeping, and moments when I've been surprised in the garden of Resurrection. They're stories both surprising and familiar, and while they're drawn from my own life, I think they'll shine at least a little light on your own desire to know Jesus. I hope my experience will be the inspiration for you to begin taking steps to meet him, get to know him, and follow where he will lead.

Think of *Follow* as a field guide, showing you a path covered with further inquiries and heartfelt answers to the questions, "Who is Jesus?" and "How can I get to know him?" If you're ready to meet Jesus and follow him with your whole heart, living in relationship with him day by day, then there are some practical, simple steps you can take and repeat that will get you closer to the one who knows you perfectly, loves you abundantly, and desires your well-being and perfection. You won't just meet Jesus once. You'll meet him again and again and be newly surprised and amazed each time by who he is, who you are, and how intense and complete his love is for you. You'll meet Jesus, get to know him, and want to follow him with your whole heart.

Meeting Jesus and being in relationship with him sets you out on a lifelong adventure, taken step by step, leaving you changed at the end of each day and for eternity. You become a pilgrim on a journey filled with twists and turns, ups and downs. Your journey in pursuit of relationship with him—the very life for which you are made—will lead you deeper and deeper into the heart of the one who sees, knows, and loves you for all that you are. Meeting him, and really getting to know him, will be the greatest experience of your life: loving and being loved by Jesus Christ. Nothing is better. Nothing is more satisfying. Nothing will bring you more joy than this lifelong adventure of following him.

Every journey has to start somewhere—so let's begin this one!

1.

LIFT YOUR HEART

The task at hand seems simple enough: get to know Jesus. It's the follow-up question that's a bit more difficult: How do we get to know him? On the surface, getting to know Jesus *should* be as simple as making friends in kindergarten.

"Hi, my name is Katie. What's yours?" was a simple enough formula in childhood, resulting in numerous friendships, some which have endured into my adulthood. But somehow, looking up at the sky and using the "Hi, my name is _____. What's yours?" approach doesn't seem useful when attempting to meet the Son of God. Maybe we should go tend sheep on a random hillside and hope a burning bush starts talking. It worked for Moses.

On the one hand, the steps on our journey to meeting Jesus in a personal, authentic way seem remarkably challenging. At the start of what looks like an endless, uphill climb, it may seem like we're trying to scale Mount Everest with nothing more than a light jacket and a pair of sneakers. On the other hand, we're reminded that there's always a first step to climbing even the tallest mountain. On the journey of coming to know Jesus, step one is to simply communicate with him the same way you would chat with a classmate, email a teacher, text a friend, yell at your parents, cry to your sister, vent to your boyfriend or girlfriend, or laugh with your teammates.

To get to know Jesus and understand who he is and why he loves you (and ultimately why you should love him back), you have to talk to him. You have to lift your heart in an authentic, heartfelt way. Let's not overcomplicate things, though. Those words still seem intimidating and this task seems huge, so let's call this what it is: lifting your heart is prayer, plain and simple. It's the first step you have to take in the epic, life-changing journey of following Jesus.

JUST NOT READY

In the spring of 2014, I dated a few guys, all in the name of good fun and searching for "the one." Nothing was very serious, but there was one standout guy I really did care a lot about and knew that for me, at least, it could become more serious. Things were going well—visits back and forth to see one another, phone calls every night, staffing a retreat together, fun and exciting dates. But after a few weeks, he ended things abruptly with a text: "I think we need to end this. You're making your way into areas of my life I'm just not ready to have anyone in yet."

There's only one place you go when your heart gets broken like that—home. I went to my mom, knowing the only place I'd feel better was with her and a tub of ice cream on the couch. A few hours of tears, *Days of Our Lives* reruns, and pints of strawberry ice cream later, I felt a little better, but I was still feeling sorry for myself.

Knowing how upset I was, but also recognizing that a motherly reality check might be in order, my mom dished out her signature brand of tough love.

"Katie, you're really upset about this, aren't you?" she asked.

"Yeah, Mom. I thought this guy was special," I mumbled through sniffly tears.

"Well, then, I just need to ask, have you prayed about this as much as you've cried about it?"

The last thing I wanted in the midst of my heartbreak was a sermon from my mom on the importance of prayer. But she had a point: If I was this distraught and tormented, why hadn't I prayed? Why hadn't I turned to the Lord in this time of hurt, distress, and trouble? In fact, if I was being honest, I couldn't really tell my mom the last time I'd prayed at all. Other than Sunday Mass and quick prayers at the start of classes each day, I hadn't spent any significant time in prayer since . . . well, probably since I'd started dating guy after guy, including the one I thought had great marriage potential. My mom was right (as she often is): I'd been crying, but I hadn't been praying. Not at all.

JESUS, I TRUST IN YOU

The pointed question my mom asked me on the couch that afternoon echoed through my head all evening, so on my way home I made a detour to Our Lady Queen of Heaven Catholic Church, the parish I'd grown up attending and deeply loved.

"Better late than never, right?" I thought to myself as I walked into the adoration chapel, finally prepared to pray more than cry. The tiny chapel was a familiar place. Twenty-four hours a day, faithful men and women come in and out of this small chapel, day after day, to pray before the Blessed Sacrament. The chapel was crammed with chairs and kneelers all placed in front of a four-foot-high stone pedestal with a monstrance resting on top. The monstrance is a sacred vessel used for exposition of the Blessed Sacrament. It is a beautiful sight and a wonderful place to sit or kneel and pray in adoration of Our Lord. I'd been inside hundreds of times in my life, but I hadn't darkened its doorstep in months. I still knew right where to sit, though, and slowly settled into my long-forgotten seat. The usual cast of characters was there: a slight, elderly lady thumbing rosary beads; a middle-aged dad in a baggy suit and loosened tie; a frazzled college student holding a notebook; and now the puffy-eyed, brokenhearted theology teacher.

It was immediately evident to me that I hadn't prayed in a long time. My heart had been closed to the Lord, and I sat there struggling to know even where to begin talking to Jesus. Despite my discomfort and confusion, I knew that this was exactly where I needed to be. I knelt down, looked up at the Blessed Sacrament, and began to cry. But this time, the tears were accompanied with prayer.

I have no idea how long I knelt there crying, but it was long enough for the elderly woman to leave and be replaced by another. Time seemed to stop as I knelt there, pouring my heart out in confusion, frustration, and pointed pleading. When I stood up, eyes still puffy and nose still stuffy, I felt better. A switch had flipped in the midst of those tears, and my restless heart had settled just a little bit. As I left the chapel, a pamphlet on top of a small table by the bathroom caught my eye. It was a small, red booklet with a black-and-white image of Jesus printed on the front under the words "The Divine Mercy." I'd certainly seen it before, but never really paid much mind to it. It was so vibrant, this image of Jesus with two rays of light bursting from his chest. The words by his feet were striking, something I obviously needed to see and believe: "Jesus, I trust in you."

"Easier said than done," I mumbled to myself. I grabbed the pamphlet, threw it on the front seat of my car, and drove home.

The sting of the abrupt text message began to dull over the next few weeks. I slowly began to forget about the guy. But there was still an ache in my heart, a void of sorts. I was lonely. I felt abandoned, broken, cast aside. Sure, he may not have turned out to be the man of my dreams, but he had been someone to talk to, lean on, and have fun with. He'd at least been there, in my life, and I missed that. I wanted someone in my life.

As my much-needed spring break from school finally arrived, I spent Good Friday morning cleaning out my car. There on the front seat, underneath piles of papers and books, was the Divine Mercy pamphlet I'd picked up just a few weeks earlier. Avoiding further spring cleaning, I opened the pamphlet and read the short history of the profound and powerful Divine Mercy chaplet. It was so simple: quick prayers said on rosary beads. But it was profound in its simplicity, so I decided I was going to pray the chaplet right there in my garage. As I settled into the passenger seat, I read the words that would change my life forever:

> The Divine Mercy chaplet is traditionally said in novena form for nine days, beginning on Good Friday and ending the Sunday after Easter, known as Divine Mercy Sunday. Each day of the novena has a specific intention that appeals to the merciful heart of Jesus. You can add your own intentions as well, asking the Lord for his abundant and perfect mercy.

Sold!

With a stack of trash piled at my feet, I resolved to pray the Divine Mercy Novena for something very specific: trust. I knew I needed to trust Jesus with my heart and my vocation. I needed to trust that Jesus had a better plan for me than I could come up with for myself. First and foremost, I knew I needed to trust in his love and let him fill the void and ache of my loneliness. My relationship with Jesus needed renewal, and this was the perfect chance to seek that out. For the next nine days, I went to the adoration chapel at my parish and prayed the chaplet. My intention became simpler and more refined each day: Help me love you, Lord. Help me believe in your plan. Jesus, help me trust in you.

Each day of the novena showed me how desperately I needed to trust Jesus with the anxiety and loneliness crippling my heart. Begging the Lord to give me a sense of trust and patience in his plan, I began to surrender my need to know everything all at once. I slowly let go of my desire to control and manage all the tiny aspects of my life. I asked for his will to be done in leading me to a companion who could help bring me closer to Jesus. I began to realize that I needed to love Jesus first so that I could love others better. More importantly, I needed to let Jesus love me, as only he could, so that I could be open to the love of others and aware of how precious I was in his eyes.

As I finished praying the chaplet on Divine Mercy Sunday that year, April 27, 2014, I heard a voice deep within me, clear as a bell: "Trust me, because I am here."

I can count on one hand the number of times I've heard the voice of Jesus. In fact, I only need one finger to do it, because it was that day. With no doubt in my mind that he had heard my prayer and was accompanying me on this journey to find fulfillment in him alone, I ended my nine days of the Divine Mercy Novena completely at peace. I'd been looking for comfort and intimacy with Jesus for a long time without really realizing that's what I'd been searching for. I'd been looking for love from others, seeking satisfaction in the impermanent things surrounding me, but there it was all along: Jesus waiting for me with open arms. This time of intentional prayer had finally awakened me to what I was made for: union with him, the one who could speak words of comfort and perfect love directly into my heart so that I could love him—and others—in a more perfect and complete way. The hurt I'd let myself wallow in after that stupid breakup had finally faded, because Jesus was here, back in the center of my life, right where he belonged. Intentional, meaningful prayer had led me right back to Jesus. My momma was right—praying is far more effective in the long run than crying.

LOOKING FOR YOU

Ten days later, on May 7, 2014, after posting a blog to my Facebook page about the joys and struggles of juggling full-time youth ministry and teaching, I received this message: "Hey, Katie! How are you doing? Thanks so much for posting that blog! I really enjoyed reading it. I've been in full-time ministry for the past two years as well, so I want you to know that I'm praying for you!"

The message was nice enough, but I was confused. It was from a guy named Tommy, whom I didn't immediately recognize. I clicked on his name and began scrolling through the album of profile pictures to try to jog my memory and see if I'd ever met him before. He didn't look familiar, but he was kind of cute. All the while, his message continued blinking at me in the bottom right-hand corner of the screen. In the time it took me to read the message, scour his pictures, and type a response, Tommy sent a winky-face emoticon to me as a follow-up to his original message. This guy was clearly flirting. I didn't know him personally, but it showed that we had more than fifty mutual Facebook friends, which meant we weren't complete strangers, and I did find him cute, so I messaged him back: "Hey, Tommy. I'm doing great, how are you? I appreciate your kind words about the blog. I'm glad someone other than my mom liked it! Where are you doing ministry?"

So began a conversation that lasted the next four hours. We talked about our jobs, our families, our time in college. He told me all about Scranton, Pennsylvania, and I described life in little Lake Charles. We swapped youth ministry stories and told each other about our favorite Shakespeare plays. We shared with each other the places we'd traveled and where we'd like to go someday. The conversation was free-flowing and easy. Before I knew it, the final bell for the end of the school day rang. I typed out a final Facebook message: "Hey, it's been great visiting with you today, but I can't live my life in a Facebook messenger box. So, guess I'll talk to you later!"

I anxiously waited for his reply, immediately wondering if what I'd said was too abrupt an end to the conversation.

He responded, "Well, I loved talking to you too. Would it be too forward of me to ask for your phone number?"

My heart fluttered with excitement as I typed my number. A few minutes later, my cell phone buzzed. Unknown number. Scranton, PA area code. The text read, "Is this the kind, beautiful, charming, funny youth minister who's had me smiling at my desk all day long?"

I blushed, then quickly replied, "Why, yes. Is this the kind, handsome, funny, charming youth director who's had ME smiling at MY desk all day long?"

He texted back, "No, this is Eugene."

This guy's got a sense of humor, I thought. I quickly typed back, "Well, if you see Tommy, can you tell him I'm looking for him?"

Moments later, he replied, "I'm pretty sure he's been looking for you for a long time too . . ."

Thus began a thirty-two-day, whirlwind, long-distance romance that eventually took me north to Scranton, Pennsylvania, to meet this Tommy guy in person. After some well-reasoned persuasion to convince my parents I wasn't crazy to fly across the country to meet a man I'd only ever spoken to on the Internet and over the phone, I hopped on a plane on June 9, 2014, and made my way halfway across the country. Those days together in Pennsylvania were nothing short of perfect. We had the chance to do all the things normal couples get to do when they live in the same town: go to dinner and a movie, hang out with friends, spend time with family. I didn't want our time together to come to an end, because I knew that any distance, especially more than a thousand miles, would be challenging to endure. So we held on to our blissful relationship vacation as long as we could.

The second-to-last-day of the visit, Tommy and I decided to spend the afternoon at his family's cottage on the banks of the Susquehanna River. Ever the romantic, Tommy set up a lovely picnic for us. As we watched the clouds roll past, we talked about our hopes and dreams and planned our next few trips to see one another. The conversation was as it had been since that first message a month before, simple and comfortable.

Spontaneously, simply because I felt so comfortable with Tommy and at ease in his presence, I asked, "What are some of your favorite ways to pray?" Prayer had righted me and set me back on course to intimacy with Jesus just weeks before Tommy and I had met. Prayer had been an anchor in the weeks that Tommy and I had gotten to know one another long distance and now in the days we were spending together. Every night that we had spoken on the phone, we had prayed together before saying goodnight. Tommy had even called me up randomly on a day that he knew I was in a bad mood and just immediately told me that he was going to pray for me right then and there, over the phone, no matter how awkward it would be. Prayer was stirring within and between us, so asking this question seemed timely, even necessary.

"Well . . ." Tommy began, caught off guard. "I really love reading scripture, especially the parables. And I usually pray a Rosary on my way to work each morning. This year I did something different, though, and I prayed the Divine Mercy Novena. I'd heard really great things about it and decided I needed to trust Jesus with my life a little more, so, yeah . . . I guess those are some of my . . . Katie, are you okay?"

My jaw had dropped in the midst of his answer, and I quickly said, "I prayed the Divine Mercy Novena this year too, and I specifically prayed to grow in trust of Jesus and to have him eventually lead me to my future spouse. I never expected it to work so quickly!"

As soon as I blurted that out, I clapped my hand over my mouth. Tommy turned white as a sheet. Oh, no. Did I just say the "spouse" word? To a guy I'd only known in person for four days and for less than forty days total? Uh-oh.

"I didn't mean to say spouse," I blurted out. "I mean, it would be great to marry you and all, and I'd love to have your children someday, but I . . ." The words just plunged out of my mouth before I even knew how to stop them. Clearly I was making it worse, because Tommy just sat there, turning whiter by the second.

"I'll be right back," Tommy mumbled as he stood up and walked toward his car. For a split second, I thought he was going to get in his Subaru and drive away, leaving me and my ridiculous spouse comments out in the middle of nowhere. First, a guy ends things over text, and now a guy runs to his car because I stupidly tell him I want to have his babies after knowing him for less than two months!

Clearly looking for something, Tommy rummaged around in his car for a few minutes. He grabbed a small black notebook out from under the passenger's seat and quickly walked back toward me. "You have to see this," he said, holding the notebook out to me, his voice quivering and hands shaking.

The entire notebook was blank, page after page empty, until I saw scratchy writing on a page in the middle. It read:

April 27, 2014: Divine Mercy Sunday
    Finished the Divine Mercy Novena today. Prayed for
my future spouse. I hope I find her soon.

I stared at the page long enough to dampen it with tears.

A CHANGED HEART

It'd be very easy to conclude that just because I prayed the Divine Mercy Novena, posted a blog on Facebook, and patiently waited for "the one," Jesus delivered this cute boy to whom I'm now married. But God is not a genie and prayers are not wishes. I did not pray then, nor should I ever pray now, just to *get* something from God. Prayer doesn't make Jesus do cool stuff in our lives. Our prayer doesn't force him to deliver good gift after good gift simply because we said the right thing, piously folded our hands, fell to our knees, and waited around to get what we wanted. That's a very childish perspective of prayer, one that places demands upon the Lord as if he's a cosmic vending machine that requires fifty-cent prayers for million-dollar miracles. "I pray, therefore I get" is the wrong attitude. Tommy and I separately entered into an intentional time of prayer in the spring of 2014. We wrote down tangible intentions and prayed specifically for companions, yes. Far more important, though, was our deep desire to grow to love, and allow ourselves to be loved by, Jesus.

Each one of us prayed for something very specific because we knew we needed significant change in our lives. That change could only be brought about by radical communion with the Lord. Our prayers were not for a ready-made relationship delivered at top speed. We prayed because we desperately needed Jesus, in a very real and tangible way, to open us up to his influence in our lives. Prayer does this. It is the avenue that allows Jesus to mold the hardened, crusty clay of our hearts *into* his heart, which is so perfect and pure and filled with his abundant love that when our hearts are swept up in his, we are changed forever. Prayer is how we enter into this intimate relationship with Jesus himself. It is not a tool to convince Jesus to do something. It is not a game of haggling in the market. We don't pray to get something from Jesus. We pray to offer him our hearts, trust, loving gratitude—our very lives. When we give him our heart, this relationship with him grows that then shapes every interaction we have with others, stabilizes and grounds every aspect of daily life, and forms us more perfectly into his disciples.

Prayer pushes us to a deeper understanding of God's perfect providence within our lives. We become who God wants us to be because we take the time to lift our hearts to him. We begin to listen and pay attention to his perfect plan, abundant love, and divine offerings. When we pray, we are formed: our hearts are readied and our intimacy with Jesus grows. We grow close to his heart when we are vulnerable and authentic with him, and we are slowly reshaped into individuals who trust God's greater plan rather than our own.

There was nothing easy about meeting, and then falling in love with, a guy who lived more than a thousand miles away. There was nothing simple about trusting that Tommy and I could make a long-distance relationship work, especially with crazy schedules, demanding jobs, and initially skeptical friends and family who wondered if we were insane for even giving this a chance. But we knew that God was in control, and we believed this wholeheartedly because of the time we'd spent talking to the Lord, sharing the depths of our hearts in prayer, and recognizing that he offers the perfect way that gives abundant life and unfailing truth. This is ultimately the fruit of prayer: to draw us near to Jesus, who gives every answer, provides unfailing care, and constantly shapes us more perfectly into his image so that we can be his likeness in the world. Prayer wasn't the cause of our relationship so much as the binding agent that kept it together, day after day. Jesus didn't give us a fairy-tale love story because we prayed for it the way little children make a wish as they toss a coin into a fountain. Prayer helped us love Jesus first, and then we were able to love each other (and many others) because of that intimacy with him. Prayer changed our hearts, because in intentional prayer we met Jesus.

Jesus cares about our hurt. He doesn't stand laughing at us, annoyed that we become sad or lonely when a promising relationship ends. He draws us close to him, giving comfort and offering peace. Jesus experienced loneliness himself as he hung upon the Cross, his friends having fled, denying they ever knew him. In prayer, we meet Jesus, who shows us again and again how precious we are to him because he takes the time to listen to us, no matter how long it takes or how confused our words may be. We discover that Jesus, the real, tangible Jesus, is not just a figure or an icon to stare at, but someone who wraps his arms around us and shows us how valuable we are to him. We come to realize that Jesus is first and foremost a very real person, and very much God. He does not stand set apart from us as some figurehead, but is in the thick and thin of life with us. In prayer we communicate with Jesus, showing him our hearts, discovering that he is truly present, listening, and relatable. We understand that Jesus wants to love us without end or interruption.

STEP BY STEP

If we try to define prayer in a simple way, we should just call it communication. It's talking and listening. Prayer is laughing, crying, shouting, fighting, whining, begging, asking, adoring, agreeing, disagreeing, and ultimately growing to understand the one who knows us better than we know ourselves. We pray to grow in communion with Jesus and be completely attuned to him. We pray so we can meet him, know him, and love him. We pray so we can be loved by him with a love that is given perfectly and without fail. If we want to know him and love him, then that requires communication, plain and simple.

Look at children who sit in sandboxes playing with plastic toys. They giggle about this or that; they babble about nothing and everything. They sit there, building tiny castles with multicolored buckets, joined in a common task. Or consider old men gathered in a barbershop. They're not there because they need trimmed the little hair they have. They are there to be with one another; the community and fellowship are the most important things. Think about your best friends, the people you share everything with. Did you text those friends today? Did you send them a Snapchat or like a picture of theirs on Instagram? Why? Were you bored? Or was it because that's what friends do? To be in communion, we need communication.

So it goes with Jesus. We sit with him, pouring our hearts out to him so we can share ourselves and come to see who he is. We share all that we are with the one who loves us completely, knowing he will sit with us and be with us as long as we need him. Our vulnerability and honesty are required for intimacy to grow. We must be patient and understanding, coming to see that sometimes his ways are not our ways and his thoughts are not our thoughts. We ask him for what we need, knowing he will provide what is best. We admit faults and failings, begging for unfailing mercy to wash over us so that we can be closer to him. We honor and adore all that he is, giving praise to his grandeur and goodness.

We do all of this, recognizing the most profound fact of all: Jesus actually wants to listen to our prayer. He wants us to be familiar with him. He wants to hear the heartfelt cries of sinful, sorrowful, confused human beings. This doesn't cheapen his divinity or lessen his power. It shows us just how important we are to him, so precious in his eyes that even the slightest whimper or the most earnest plea is met with a response of love and Jesus' perfect and complete attention.

Prayer begins to help us realize that Jesus isn't a distant fairy-tale figure existing in a Christian storybook. He's not a far-off character with mythical, miraculous powers waiting to grant us wishes, nor is he a pop psychologist with feel-good phrases to boost our egos. Jesus is the lover of our soul, who cares more deeply about us than anyone else possibly could. He wants us to share the depths of our heart so he can reach us even there. Prayer is how we let him into our lives. Prayer is step one.

Knowing this is the essential first step can be a bit daunting. You may not know what to say in prayer, where to begin, or whether or not you're doing it right. Try to move beyond thinking of prayer merely as a task to be completed if you want to be a good Christian. Prayer is a movement; it's a step forward on this journey toward Jesus. So let's do this. Let's learn how to pray.

SPONTANEOUS PRAYER

First things first. Talking to Jesus isn't as convenient or seemingly simple as talking with or texting a friend or loved one. That's easy because we can see them or hear them right away. But spontaneous prayer or casual conversation with the Lord can and should be just as familiar and comfortable as conversation with your family or friends. I text my best friends when something makes me laugh. I call my mom when I need comfort or advice. I discuss big decisions with my husband. So too must I turn to Jesus and simply share with him what is on my heart and mind.

Pay attention to certain things you notice, experience, and feel during the day, and talk to Jesus about these things. He is there to listen; you just have to start the conversation. Get into the habit of beginning a conversation with Jesus by addressing him directly, vulnerably, and authentically. Slowly, you'll become familiar with talking to him, just as you have with the people you see every day. Don't worry about whether or not what you're saying is pretty or poetic. Messy and jumbled is just as beautiful, because it's you sharing yourself, and you are probably messy and jumbled too.

- Starting today, take note of all the moments of grace empowering you throughout the day: the compassion you feel toward someone who is struggling, the desire to help someone in need, the ability to notice another's acts of kindness. Each "grace moment" you notice (and you'll become more aware of these as time goes on), stop and say, "Thank you, Jesus, for . . ." or "Jesus, you are wonderful because . . ."
- Tomorrow, focus on talking to Jesus about what is weighing on your mind and causing you worry and fear. When you feel stuck in a rut, ask Jesus to aid you in wisdom and understanding, saying, "Jesus, help me to . . ." or "Jesus, guide me in . . ." In the same vein, as you notice moments of anxiety and pain, lean on Jesus and ask him to pour peace and serenity into your heart, saying, "Jesus, give me patience with . . ." or "Jesus, calm me as I . . ."
- Take one day and pay attention to all the moments when you feel proud and excited and then purposefully acknowledge Jesus' good work in your life. Thank him by saying, "Jesus, you have helped me to . . ." or "Jesus, I am in awe of the way you . . ."

- Spend a day acknowledging every good gift you are given throughout the day, whether it is help with homework, an act of mercy from a teacher, or an encouraging word from a friend. Big or small, these gifts are opportunities to express authentic gratitude by saying, "Jesus, I am grateful that . . ." or "Jesus, because of you I have . . ."
- Take one day to think of all the specific areas in which you need help and assistance. Each time you feel stunted or in need of aid, especially with the issues that only seem to build and grow, talk to Jesus, saying "Give me strength to . . ." or "Jesus, help me with . . ."

After a few days of focusing on specific experiences and moments, it will become easier to just spontaneously begin talking to Jesus. On the way to class, you may mentally ask him for help to be able to study for and do well on an upcoming test. On the drive home from school, you might naturally begin to thank him for the blessings you were given throughout the day. While headed to hang out with friends, you may find yourself talking to Jesus about your hopes for the evening and ask him to help you be a good friend to all those you're going to spend time with. In a moment of tragedy or hurt, you'll find it easier to turn to Jesus and ask for comfort and aid in your brokenness and pain. Spontaneous prayer is an authentic conversation with Jesus, opening your heart in a natural way and beginning to simply talk to him.

FAMILIAR FAVORITES

Most of us were taught to pray in a very rote, repetitive way, which is good. It's like learning the alphabet by singing the ABC's song over and over again. But we don't want to fall into the trap of thinking that prayer is just recitation of familiar words and phrases. Certain memorized prayers with specific rhythms were probably drilled into your head, and you could say them in your sleep. Use those familiar prayers to your advantage: they're a great starting place when learning how to work consistent, authentic communication with Jesus into your life. Even some rote prayers that may be lesser known can be added to your arsenal to help you cry out to Jesus with an open and honest heart.

The Our Father

These are the very words Jesus taught the apostles when they asked him how to pray. You may know these well, but I'm quite certain some of you don't.

> Our Father, who art in Heaven, hallowed be thy name.
> Thy Kingdom come, thy will be done,
> on earth as it is in heaven.
> Give us this day, our daily bread, and forgive us our trespasses,
> as we forgive those who trespass against us;
> and lead us not into temptation, but deliver us from evil.
> Amen.

Each line of the Our Father can be broken down and a wealth of meaning unpacked with each phrase, giving you plenty to think about when it comes to your relationship with Jesus and what's going on in your life. Take time to write out the Our Father, rewriting each line of the prayer in your own words once you've pondered its meaning. It's impossible to spend too much time with the very prayer Jesus taught us, so become familiar with each line and how it uniquely applies to your life and your growing relationship with the Lord. These questions may help:

- What does it mean to you, right now, to ask the Lord to give you daily bread?
- How has God shown himself to be your father day by day?
- Have you truly forgiven others? If not, what grudges are you holding on to that you need to release?

The Hail Mary

A beautiful and poetic articulation of the identity, holiness, and role of God's own Mother, the Hail Mary is the premier Catholic prayer.

> Hail Mary, full of grace, the Lord is with thee;
> blessed art thou among women,
> and blessed is the fruit of thy womb, Jesus.
> Holy Mary, Mother of God, pray for us sinners now
> and at the hour of our death.
> Amen.

The first half of the Hail Mary is drawn from the Bible. These are words used to greet and describe Mary during the Annunciation of Jesus' birth in the Gospel of Luke (Lk 1:26–39) and the visitation to her cousin Elizabeth (Lk 1:39–56). The second half of the prayer is our petition, when we ask Mary to pray for us and lead us closer to the heart of her Son, whom she knows better than anyone else.

Think about the descriptive phrases used in reference to Mary and the way her identity is a model for our own attempts to become holy. Go line by line through the prayer, as with the Our Father, and consider the deeper meaning behind the words we often say so casually and quickly.

- Mary is "full of grace." How? How does she show us throughout her life to avoid sin ourselves? How does she model complete and perfect sanctity, both in the moments of the Annunciation and throughout her life?
- The Lord is with Mary. Is Jesus with you? Do you pay attention to him throughout your day? Do you turn to him for comfort, advice, guidance, or to show gratitude?
- Mary is blessed among women, held in high esteem because of the child she carries in her womb. What blessings, both big and small, have been given to you? How have you responded to these blessings and allowed them to shape and mold you into a follower of Jesus?
- How might you, like Mary, be a bearer of Christ to our world?

The Glory Be

A simple, quick, straightforward little prayer, the Glory Be is comfortable and familiar and easy, but it packs a punch in only thirty words.

> Glory be to the Father, and to the Son, and to the Holy Spirit.
> As it was in the beginning, is now, and ever shall be,
> world without end.
> Amen.

Think about the intensity of this short prayer: The Father, the Son, and the Holy Spirit are called upon. God is a Trinity, a perfect communion, unified and distinct. This great mystery of the Trinity is worth contemplating, because we can ponder God's immense power. This prayer reminds us that God is outside of time: what was in the beginning, happens now, and will come to pass in the future are all one moment for the eternal Creator who is not bound by the limits of the watches we wear or the calendars we fill.

- What does it mean to you to give glory to our God, who is three persons in one? How do you praise God by the way you live? In what ways do you relate to God as father or loving parent? In what moments have you noticed the saving power of the Son? In what ways do you let the Holy Spirit guide you?
- Are you busy? Do you fill up your days with tasks that cause you stress?
- What worries you? Have you asked God to help alleviate your anxiety and give you calm?
- Do you try to overly control every situation in your life to the point of forgetting that God is in charge? What can you do to return to a place of peace and understanding that the eternal God is in control and should be trusted?

The Universal Prayer

I first encountered this prayer in college when I found it in a small prayer book in the chapel on my college's campus in Rome, Italy.

Attributed to Pope Clement XI, the prayer is a wonderful meditation after receiving Holy Communion. It's long, but it really does cover all the bases and forces us to think about nearly every aspect of life and our relationship with Jesus.

Lord, I believe in you; grant me stronger faith.
I trust in you; give me a more confident hope.
I love you; may I love you more ardently.
I am sorry for my sins; may I have a deeper sorrow.

I worship you as my first beginning;
I long for you as my last end.
I praise you as my constant helper
and invoke you as my gracious protector.

Guide me by your wisdom,
Correct me with your justice,
Comfort me with your kindness,
Protect me with your power.

I offer you, Lord, my thoughts, that they may rise to you;
My words, that they may speak of you;
My actions, that they may follow your will;
My sufferings, that they may be borne for you.

I will whatever you will:
I will all because you will it;
I will all things to be as you wish them;
I will them as long as you will them.

Lord, enlighten my understanding,
Inflame my will,
Purify my heart,
And sanctify my soul.

Help me repent of my past sins
and put to flight future temptations.
Make me conquer my evil inclinations
and cultivate the virtues I should have.
Grant that I may love you, O good God, and despise myself.

May I have zeal for my neighbor and contempt for the world.
May I strive to obey my superiors
and to assist those dependent on me;
Make me solicitous of my friends,
And happy to spare my enemies.

Help me to master pleasure-seeking by austerity,
Greed by generosity,
Anger by gentleness,
And apathy by fervor.

Make me prudent in my plans,
Courageous in times of danger,
Patient in suffering,
And unassuming in prosperity.

Keep me, Lord, attentive at prayer,
Temperate in food and drink,
Diligent in my work,
And firm in my good intentions.

Let my inner life be innocent and my outer behavior modest.
Let my speech be blameless and my life well-ordered.

May I take care to master my natural impulses;
Let me cherish growth in grace.
May I keep your law, and come at last to win salvation.

Teach me to realize how slight are earthly things
and how great is that which is divine,
How swiftly things oft time pass,
And how enduring are eternal realities.

Help me prepare for death and have a right fear of judgment;
May I escape hell and take possession of heaven.
Grant this through Christ, our Lord. Amen.

The Prayer of St. Francis of Assisi

This repetitive, comforting prayer compares the things of this world with the virtues of the Lord. It's a simple and lovely prayer to use at the end of each day, especially if you first examine your conscience and name the ways you struggled to live your faith and love Jesus. This prayer can lead you to ask for forgiveness and guidance to do better the next day.

Lord, make me an instrument of your peace:
Where there is hatred, let me sow love;
Where there is injury, pardon;
Where there is doubt, faith;
Where there is despair, hope;
Where there is darkness, light;
Where there is sadness, joy.

O divine Master, grant that I may not so much seek to be
    consoled as to console,
To be understood as to understand,
To be loved as to love.
For it is in giving that we receive,
It is in pardoning that we are pardoned,
And it is in dying that we are born to eternal life.
Amen.

The Litany of Humility

I affectionately call this prayer "the prayer that must not be prayed" unless you're ready for the Lord to really change your life. Attributed to Cardinal Merry del Val, this simple litany is a powerful, life-changing prayer that forces you to think about how God is God and you are not. It's a chance to truly bring to Jesus your desire to be formed in his image, not your own, and to trust that he will refine your soul as he sees fit. But be careful, this prayer is sure to challenge you, especially when you least expect it. I pray this prayer when I'm facing a big decision, holding a position of power or leadership, and becoming egotistical and foolishly prideful.

O Jesus! Meek and humble of heart, Hear Me.

Response: Deliver me, Jesus
From the desire of being esteemed . . .
From the desire of being extolled . . .
From the desire of being honored . . .
From the desire of being praised . . .
From the desire of being preferred to others . . .
From the desire of being consulted . . .
From the desire of being approved . . .
From the fear of being humiliated . . .
From the fear of being despised . . .
From the fear of suffering rebukes . . .
From the fear of being calumniated . . .
From the fear of being forgotten . . .
From the fear of being ridiculed . . .
From the fear of being wronged . . .
From the fear of being suspected . . .

Response: Jesus, grant me the grace to desire it
That others may be loved more than I . . .
That others may be esteemed more than I . . .
That in the opinion of the world others may increase and I
    may decrease . . .
That others may be chosen and I set aside . . .
That others may be praised and I unnoticed . . .
That others may be preferred to me in everything . . .
That others become holier than I, provided that I become as
    holy as I should . . .
Amen.

The Book of Psalms

The psalms are sort of like the Bible's prayer book and are found in the Old Testament (the first half of sacred scripture). They're really kind of smack-dab in the middle of the Bible, after the book of Job and before the book of Proverbs. Attributed to King David, these are prayers and hymns of praise, petition, exaltation, sorrow, lament, joy, and relief. David was a shepherd, warrior, king, sinner, and saint. These prayers from his heart allow us to see how familiar and relatable much of his life is, and each psalm can help us enter into deep, personal conversation with Jesus.

Read one a night, starting at the beginning and working your way through them in order. Highlight or underline the words and phrases that stand out to you in each psalm and look for a pattern and theme to emerge.

- What words, phrases, or images catch your attention?
- What are you drawn to thinking about when you read this psalm? Why do you think that is?
- How are these words of King David prompting you to speak to Jesus?

Powerful Beads

What's more Catholic than the Rosary? Probably just the pope, and even he is praying the Rosary. When I was a kid, I thought the Rosary was boring. I had no true understanding of the recitation of the same prayer fifty times while thumbing small beads that could easily be repurposed as a whip with which to hit my little sister. It was something for old ladies to do before Mass, and you prayed the Rosary for people when they died, but that's all I thought it was.

The creation of the Rosary is attributed to St. Dominic, who received a vision of Mary and then taught this simple method of prayer to the people to whom he was ministering. It's straightforward and simple, just a recitation of the three most familiar Catholic prayers: the Our Father, Hail Mary, and Glory Be. Each prayer is said on a bead that is collected into a decade. Five decades equal one Rosary. But it isn't meant to serve as just some Catholic activity to check off one's prayer to-do list each day. The beads of the rosary, and the familiar prayers said on each one, are meant to help us enter into the very mystery of Jesus' life. An entire Rosary, five decades, takes a set of mysteries and looks at certain moments from the life of Christ. These episodes from his life, which are just as familiar as the prayers we are saying, can help us more fully enter into an understanding of who Jesus is, what he did during his time on earth, and how we can better model our own lives on his. Each mystery of the Rosary has a reference point in the Bible, so when you pray the Rosary, it can be helpful to also read the passage associated with that particular mystery.

The Joyful Mysteries

These mysteries focus on some of the most familiar and well-known moments from Jesus' birth and childhood.

- The Annunciation (Luke 1:35)
- The Visitation (Luke 1:39–56)
- The Nativity of Our Lord (Luke 2:1–20)
- The Presentation in the Temple (Luke 2:22–24)
- The Finding of the Child Jesus in the Temple (Luke 2:41–52)

The Luminous Mysteries

Introduced by St. John Paul II, these mysteries consider Jesus' public miracles and teachings, helping us to meditate on his divine action on earth.

- The Baptism of Jesus by John in the River Jordan (Luke 3:21–22)
- The Wedding Feast at Cana (John 2:1–12)
- The Proclamation of the Kingdom with the Call to Conversion (Matthew 9:35)
- The Transfiguration of Our Lord (Luke 9:28–36)
- The Institution of the Holy Eucharist (Mark 14:17–25)

The Sorrowful Mysteries

These mysteries bring us to the Cross as we walk to Calvary, contemplating the suffering and pain Jesus went through for our salvation.

- The Agony in the Garden (Luke 22:44)

- The Scourging at the Pillar (John 19:1)
- The Crowning with Thorns (John 19:2)
- The Carrying of the Cross (John 19:17)
- The Crucifixion (John 17:18)

The Glorious Mysteries

These mysteries help us see the Lord's great triumph as we think about the glory of the Resurrection and what God does in his victory over death.

- The Resurrection of Jesus (Luke 24:6)
- The Ascension (Acts 1:9–11)
- The Descent of the Holy Spirit (Acts 2:1–13)
- The Assumption of Our Lady (1 Corinthians 15:22–23)
- The Coronation of Our Lady as Queen of Heaven and Earth (Revelation 12:1)

Each mystery meditated on while praying the Rosary may be a familiar story to you, but each one is worth contemplating time and again. In this way, you can get to know Jesus better, see the meaning of his life more clearly, and allow yourself to be drawn into the great beauty of what he did, said, and experienced. Read the passage associated with each mystery and contemplate the moment so that you can be drawn into the life of Jesus as you pray the familiar words of this great devotion.

INTENTIONAL PETITIONS

A few years ago, I began keeping a small journal with me throughout the day. It easily fits in my pocket, purse, or backpack. It's unmarked, with nothing written on the front, because it's what's inside that is significant. In this little notebook I write down various intentions and short prayers that pop into my head throughout the day. Sometimes it's just a name or a very short phrase, things such as "Mrs. Stroud: cancer" or "Dawson family buying new house." Sometimes it's random petitions or moments I don't want to forget: "Grateful for the smile from Claudia" or "Need patience with Owen." Often times it's just a single word: "perseverance" or "hope."

Think about how busy you are throughout the day. Juggling school, athletics, extracurricular activities, family obligations, and just attempting to have a social life is enough to clutter your head and cause you to easily forget even the simplest things you want to talk to Jesus about. A little notebook can help ensure that the busyness doesn't distract you from what you need to bring to Jesus. Get a notebook and begin carrying it around with you. These prompts and tips can help you begin taking advantage of the intentional practice of writing down your prayers.

- Make a list of all the people you know who are facing some sort of struggle right now: maybe they're sick or facing a big decision. Do you know anyone who doubts their faith or has a grudge against Jesus? Who in your life seems to be worried or anxious? Write down their names with a simple reminder of what's going on in their lives and follow it up with what to say to God on their behalf.
- Throughout the day, when situations cause you stress or anxiety, jot down a short phrase to remind you to offer this up to Jesus. Maybe you have a big test coming up or you're in the midst of completing college applications. Perhaps you had a huge fight with a parent or you lost your temper with a sibling. If it's in your head, then it's a valuable practice to write it down so that it doesn't continue to bother or distract you. Whatever weighs on your mind is worth bringing to Jesus, who will provide comfort and aid.
- When situations arise, both good and bad, what would help you best approach and handle that moment? Do you need a spirit of peace and a sense of calm? Should you be more trusting of the Lord? Are you struggling to be resilient and perseverant? Is there a need to be grateful and joyful? Write down the virtues and attitudes that you need to help strengthen your relationship with Jesus.

My prayer time is more fruitful when I use the things written down in my little notebook as my prayer prompts. I'm more focused and know exactly where to begin and what to say, and then I'm able to take the time to sit and say it. Writing these things down can help you stay diligent and attuned to your constant need to pray. You won't forget things and you'll form a good habit of how much you need to pray and for whom.

THE A.C.T.S. METHOD OF PRAYER

There's a very helpful method of prayer that cycles through four "movements" whenever you take intentional time to talk to Jesus. Dubbed the A.C.T.S. Method, it's a four-step model of what to be sure to include when you pray. It's a great system of checks and balances for the variety of things we have to say to the Lord, especially if we find ourselves leaning far too heavily on asking him for stuff or just whining about our struggles (which is totally allowed but not all we should be doing). The A.C.T.S. Method is a sequential movement as you go to the Lord with a humble heart, open mind, and ready spirit. Going through the sequence, in order, whether for five minutes or an hour, is a chance to truly commune with Jesus, growing in intimacy with him. You share your heart, and you begin to experience his.

Adoration: God Is God, I Am Not, and Thank God for That!

Right from the start, it has to be acknowledged that God is greater and far more powerful than us. He is God, after all, Creator of the Universe, not contained by time, purveyor of all gifts, and master of all that is good and holy. We need to go to him and recognize this power. Easier said than done, right? We throw that line around, "go to God," as if it's easy to do—as if we can just sit down and start chatting with the Creator, face-to-face. While you can't necessarily *see* him as you might see your best friend or your mail carrier, you can clear your mind and place yourself in his presence. Quiet yourself and begin to concentrate on God's very presence in this moment.

- Remove distractions that could throw you off: silence your phone, turn off the TV and computer, close your notebooks, and put away homework. Close your eyes. Take a few deep breaths and ask the Lord to fill the space, awaken your mind, and bring comfort to your soul. If anything is worrying you, causing stress or anxiety, acknowledge it for what it is ("I have a ton of homework to finish today"). Try to move beyond it. The homework will still be there when you're done, but for this time, you are sitting in God's presence and trying to focus on him.

- Once your mind is clear, begin to think about who God is. Start by listing off various attributes of God, such as "God, you are powerful" or "Lord, you are strong." Be intentional and specific in describing him, because when we acknowledge *who* he is and see that in his great power he still loves us, then we are able to continue approaching him with an open heart and mind.

- This time of adoration when you acknowledge his power, glory, might, and being is meant to give you perspective on how great he is in comparison to how small we are. End this first movement by saying something such as "God, I adore you in your might, I praise you in your power, and I am in awe and wonder at your glory. Show me yourself more so that I may delight in your goodness. Amen."

Contrition: Forgive Me, for I Have Run from You

God is God. You've acknowledged that in your first movement and are aware of his immense and awesome power. You've placed yourself in his presence and taken note of his goodness. It should become abundantly clear, then, that there are times and moments when you have failed to place yourself in his presence—when you have stumbled and fallen into sin. When we do what we want, giving in to selfish desires and failing to pay attention to and follow God's will over our own will, we sin. Sin is the attempt to become our own god, controlling things ourselves rather than being conformed to Christ.

The Ten Commandments are the blueprints of how we should live our lives. When we fail to uphold them, and when we know we have ignored them, we can pinpoint the specific moments of sin for which we must express sorrow and ask forgiveness. In this second movement of the A.C.T.S. Method, we approach the all-powerful, loving God and ask him to forgive us of our sins. We acknowledge the ways we tried to become God on our own and ask him to take us back, heal our hearts, and cleanse us with his abundant mercy so that we can return to intimacy and union with him. As you meditate on the Ten Commandments, be specific and purposeful in articulating how you have walked away from God and why you want to return to him.

Take a moment and think through the Ten Commandments, one by one.

- First Commandment: Did you make other things (money, friends, school, status) more important than God?
- Second Commandment: Did you curse excessively or use God's name casually or without reverence?
- Third Commandment: Did you skip Mass on Sunday for no good reason?

- Fourth Commandment: Did you disobey your parents or authority figures?
- Fifth Commandment: Did you steal, cheat, lie, slander, gossip, drink, do drugs, or harm yourself or others?
- Sixth Commandment: Were you lustful or impure in thought or deed? Did you treat yourself or another person like an object?
- Seventh Commandment: Did you take things that weren't yours?
- Eighth Commandment: Did you lie or spread falsehoods? Did you gossip?
- Ninth and Tenth Commandments: Were you jealous or envious to the point of wishing ill upon another?

This is by no means an exhaustive examination of conscience, but it can help get the wheels turning and make you aware of ways you've stumbled and how you need to get back to the Lord. As you go through these questions and express a true desire to repent and be drawn back to God, make a commitment to receive the sacrament of Reconciliation so that you can receive his abundant mercy and healing grace.

Thanksgiving: My Attitude of Gratitude in the Presence of Jesus

We have adored the Lord's glory and begged for (and received) his mercy. God is good. He is worthy of being praised and thanked for all that he has provided, is giving us now, and will continue to deliver in the future. In this third movement, express your gratitude to him. Think about specific blessings, big or small, and then name them, showing that you are aware of the lavish love the Lord bestows upon you. We give thanks because we know he provides and will continue to provide. We know he is powerful, we know we have sinned, failing at times to trust and live in his goodness, and so we ask for his forgiveness. Now we express gratitude for that and much more.

- List the things for which you are grateful, just from this day. You may have had a great conversation with a friend or done well on a test. It could be as simple as being grateful that you were in a good mood on the way to school or as profound as having received good news that someone has recovered from an illness. Specifically say the words, "Thank you, Jesus" as you think of each blessing in your life.
- Begin to think more broadly with your list: What are you grateful for from this past week? Month? Year?
- In what areas of your life have you experienced blessings? In school? With family? At work? With friends? With enemies?
- When have you experienced struggles? Have those times of distress strengthened you and helped you rely more heavily on Jesus?
- Are you grateful for all that he provides, whether you understand it or not?

Supplication: Jesus, Supply Me with . . .

We can go to the Lord, with faith and trust in his immense power that we have experienced and acknowledged, and ask him to supply us with what we need. It's not just a matter of simply asking because you want something. You aren't wishing upon his will the same way Jiminy Cricket told Pinocchio to wish upon a star. You turn to the Lord and ask for his action in your life, trusting ultimately in his great plan and believing his will is good above all things. Notice, we don't ask Jesus for anything (or beg him to supply us with *more* good things) until after we have acknowledged his power, recognized our sinfulness, and expressed gratitude for what has already been given. This is the final movement of the A.C.T.S. Method precisely because our attitude toward prayer shouldn't be one of "What can I get?" but rather "Who is Jesus and how can I love him more by offering my heart up to him?"

- Specifically list or name things you're struggling with. Identify people who need to be lifted up. Acknowledge moments of conflict or strife that need healing. If you began keeping an intentional prayer journal and list (as suggested above), this is the perfect time to pull it out and begin going through it.

- If someone is sick, pray for him or her by name. If a situation is bothering you, ask Jesus to bring patience and peace into those moments. If an assignment is looming, ask Jesus for focus and studiousness. If you are lonely or afraid, ask Jesus to make you more aware of his presence and love in your life. If you see a friend hurt or a loved one in pain, ask Jesus to bring them comfort and hope.

The A.C.T.S. Method of prayer is tangible, simple, and straightforward. Become familiar with the steps, going deeper into each movement every time so that you can more intensely connect with Jesus and grow closer to him.

EVER CLOSER

Every evening, as Tommy and I get ready for bed, we find ourselves talking about the day's events. Sometimes we're standing at the sink, brushing our teeth, or we're packing the next day's lunches in the kitchen. When we have time, we sit on the couch, turn off our phones, and only focus on each other and our conversation, catching up and simply sharing. What we say isn't profound or life changing. Most nights, it's fairly mundane and boring. We're just a normal married couple recounting funny moments or annoying instances from the day. Sometimes it's stuff we've already talked about, but I love that boring conversation at the end of our day. It's one of my favorite things, not because of its profundity or complexity, but because it's just the two of us sharing our hearts as we bond over simple moments, discuss decisions, offer advice, provide comfort, and grow closer together. If we want to get to know Jesus and grow close to his heart, we have to do the same thing with him. We must communicate with him, lifting our hearts in simple, heartfelt prayer.

2.

OPEN YOUR EARS

Step by step, we learn to pray and develop the necessary skill of authentic communication with Jesus, sharing who we are deep down in our souls. We also come to understand who he is. But that's easier said than done, right? We're expected to talk to Jesus to get to know him, but we can't see him or even hear his voice. It can feel as if we're speaking into the void: "Hi, Jesus, it's me, Katie. Are you there?" Then we just wait for a reply, which we believe will come, but not necessarily right away or in the manner we expected. Prayer is just the first movement of our journey of following Jesus. We're setting out on a *lifelong* adventure with Jesus, not a quick stroll along a short trail that ends as quickly as it began. We're getting to know Jesus. We're meeting him face-to-face, and over time we will become unafraid to simply approach him with the thoughts, longings, desires, hurts, joys, sufferings, and moments of our daily lives.

But is that all we're supposed to do with Jesus—just talk and talk and wait for some response? Prayer isn't just some monologue, listing our grievances, outlining our wishes, or presenting our needs. It's an authentic lifting of the heart whereby we intimately commune and grow in relationship with Jesus. And that's the hard part: waiting for, and listening to, his response. It's easy to begin wondering if he's even there.

I went on a retreat as a senior in high school, a mandatory day of reflection that most of us didn't want to be at and thought was a gigantic waste of time. We weren't wrong, since most of the day was spent drawing a picture that "captured our senior year" and mocking the speaker who burst into tears every five minutes as she gave her overly emotional talk. Finally, as the day was drawing to a close, one of the teachers took the microphone and decided to lead us in a final meditation to end the day. "Just close your eyes and listen for Jesus' voice," he said. I started laughing to myself quietly as I began to imagine what Jesus' voice sounded like. Was it deep and booming, like the voice that introduces the evening news? Or was it high-pitched and warbled, like an annoying cartoon character? Either way, I wasn't hearing any version of it while my classmates and I sat there with our eyes closed, waiting for the final bell to ring so we could leave.

Just because we can't hear Jesus' voice in the way we hear other loved ones' voices, though, doesn't mean he's not speaking to us. Jesus speaks in the very depths of our hearts and in our thoughts. This means a different sort of listening is required of us than the way we listen to others. Jesus responds in some manner to our every cry, whether pitiful or powerful. He listens to us and invites us to listen to him, and it's when we pick up the very Word of God—the sacred scriptures given to us—that we are immersed in his voice. It's there that he shows us his abundant love and speaks to the depths of our hearts.

EARLY MORNING WAKE-UP

"Katie . . . hey, Katie. Get up. Baby, come on, get up."

Groggily I rolled over in my bed and looked at my alarm clock. It was 4:30 a.m., far too early for my mom to be standing by my bed, shaking me awake. She was frantic, clearly distressed and upset.

"Hurry up. Come on, you need to wake up. Katie, we have to pack. We've got to leave."

I sat up in my bed, propping myself up on the pillows as I rubbed sleep out of my eyes, disoriented and confused.

"What's going on? Where are we going? Mom, what's wrong?" I mumbled, still trying to get my bearings.

"The storm, Katie. The hurricane. The governor ordered a mandatory evacuation and we have to leave Lake Charles. It shifted slightly overnight and it's going to make landfall in Cameron and then come up to us. We have to leave in the next couple hours."

As I gradually became more awake and aware of what was happening, things started to click. Hurricane Rita, a storm forming in the Gulf of Mexico over the prior few days, had picked up strength as the warm waters churned. The humid air coming off the coast had only served as more fuel, and the storm was now classified as a Category 5 hurricane, set to make landfall sometime within the next thirty-six hours.

"We're going to your grandparents' house, but we have to hurry and pack up some stuff. Dad is boarding the windows now and I'm getting all the papers together. I need you and Laura to fill these up with anything you think is irreplaceable. Can you do that?"

There at the end of my bed sat an empty forty-gallon plastic bin, the lid propped up inside.

"Can you do that, Katie? I need you to tell me you can help me with that."

My mom was beginning to tear up as she stared at me, so I quickly responded, "Yes, ma'am, yes. I can do that. When are we leaving? Is Laura up yet?" Mom said we had about two hours to get everything together, and she left my room to go wake up my little sister.

I sat in my bed for another few minutes, scanning my bedroom. It was filled with my most prized possessions and a good amount of stuff I probably didn't need. A shelf held the porcelain dolls my Uncle Tony had given me for my birthday each year. Next to the dolls was the small collectible copy of *The Tale of Peter Rabbit* that my Grandma Rose had given me. There was a stack of school textbooks sitting on my desk, my backpack open on the floor with incomplete math homework stuffed haphazardly inside. My dresser was covered in headbands and hair ties, half-used makeup, and hairbrushes. My plaid school skirt was hanging on the doorknob of my closet, my Sperry boat shoes tossed next to it. The disorganized bookshelf was covered with my favorite books and a few picture frames filled with photos from youth group retreats, mission trips, and family vacations. I hopped out of bed, grabbed my Harry Potter books, and put them in the bin. Then I stepped back to the doorway, surveying the room completely. I started throwing things into the bin randomly—my baptismal certificate framed and hung on the wall, a photo of my best friend and me, a rock from a trail in the Great Smoky Mountains, a poster of my favorite band, my school shoes. The items were random, some significant and others tossed in out of a sense of obligation. After a few minutes, I heard soft cries coming from my sister's room, so I walked down the hall to try to help her pack. She was sitting on the floor, twelve years old, in a puddle of tears, clutching her American Girl Bitty Baby Doll.

"Katie, am I too old to take this? I just don't want it to be gone if the house blows away, and Mom gave it to me . . ." She choked back more tears as she placed the baby doll in her bin, along with more random items from her room. We walked downstairs together half an hour later, our bins packed, eyes puffy from crying. Dad was loading things into his gigantic Ford Excursion, which he had always jokingly called his "hurricane evacuation vehicle." Mom was taking paintings off the walls, wrapping them in blankets, and placing them in the playroom upstairs. Her logic was simple: if the water got high enough, then at least they'd be on the second floor. As she was instructing Laura to take all the framed family photos and place them in another bin, Dad frantically rushed inside.

"Marie, if you put stuff upstairs, it'll get ruined if the roof comes off! At least the house is up on piers . . . there's no way water will get higher than eight feet. Right?"

And that's when Mom began to cry. We all just stood there in the living room, surrounded by bins filled with a hodgepodge of items we saw every single day but had never really thought we'd have to pack up to ensure they weren't lost forever. With no idea of what this Category 5 storm was going to bring, we emptied out the fridge, packed up the dog and cat, secured plywood boards on the windows, loaded up the vehicles, and began our two-hour drive north to Alexandria, Louisiana. We were leaving behind the only home I'd ever really known.

I was riding with Mom, sitting shotgun in her powder blue Volkswagen Beetle, the dog and cat securely tucked into the back seat in their crates. Convinced it was going to start raining any minute, Laura had insisted on riding with Dad in the Excursion so she didn't drown when the streets began to flood. As we pulled out of the driveway, I turned around in my seat and looked out the back window at the big white house I'd lived in since I was five years old. The large columns set across the front porch looked majestic, glimmering in the early morning sunlight. The tall pine trees surrounding the house normally swayed in the wind, but they were eerily still as the orange sky cast a chilling glow across the sky. Mom was silently crying, a rosary clutched in her hand as she gripped the steering wheel with all her might.

Suddenly, I cried out, "Wait, Mom! Dad left his shoes on the front porch!"

"Oh, those ratty old things he wears for yard work? Just leave them. Maybe they'll get washed away and I'll never have to see those ugly, smelly things again. You know those things are practically older than you. Maybe it'll take a hurricane to convince him to buy a new pair."

CONSTANT COVERAGE

The normally two-hour drive took us closer to six and a half. We stopped twice to fuel up the gas tanks, Dad buying gas cans at each station and filling them to the brim. "For the generator," he said each time. Mom and I rode in relative silence for most of the trip, occasionally pointing out very obvious things we saw along the way. "Oh, wow, they brought a trailer for their stuff" and "I wonder if those trees will be here next week." The cat meowed quietly in the back seat and our little Chihuahua shook in her little crate, clearly afraid of what was going on. We moved slowly up through central Louisiana, along with thousands of other people filling the highways, looking to get as far away from the coast as possible. As we pulled into my grandparents' driveway, close to one o'clock in the afternoon, a wave of exhaustion hit us both as I said, "I feel like the whole day is already over and we haven't even had lunch yet . . ."

We hopped out of the cars, eyes bloodshot and red from exhaustion and crying. Laura immediately ran over to Mom, grabbing her around the waist and smothering her head in her stomach. Dad began lining up his filled gas cans under the carport. My grandparents came out of the house and met us in the driveway, smiles plastered across their faces. Even in the midst of impending doom—what I considered the veritable apocalypse barreling toward us with hundred-mile-an-hour winds under the name of Rita—my grandma's warm smile and Papa's hearty laugh calmed me down. They pulled us into hugs, gave us updates on the movement of the storm from what they'd seen on the Weather Channel, and then insisted it was time to eat. We grabbed our suitcases, unpacked the pets, and then filled our plates with Grandma's home cooking—mashed potatoes, corn bread, fried chicken, and green beans. In the middle of a storm, Cajuns eat. A cake just pulled from the oven was waiting to be iced.

If not for the steady background drone of the Weather Channel's Jim Cantore giving analysis on the track of the storm, this was just a normal gathering at Grandma and Papa's house. We scarfed down our food, realizing just how hungry and tired we all were. Mom suggested Laura and I go unpack our bags and lie down to take a nap. After we both insisted we were fine, she told us to take the dog for a walk or go watch TV in the other room. It became evident that Mom and Dad wanted us to leave the room so they could talk to Grandma and Papa. Catching the hint, I convinced Laura to watch a movie with me in Papa's office and we left the adults sitting at the kitchen counter. As we walked down the hall, I heard my mom deeply sigh, saying, "I honestly don't know if the house is going to be there by the weekend, Momma. We may be here a while."

The next few hours felt like an entire week. We sat in front of the television all day, flipping back and forth between CNN and the Weather Channel, watching updates as the storm made landfall in the wee hours of the morning. Winds were one hundred and twenty miles per hour. The storm surge from the lake was hitting the city with an intensity the likes of which none of the reporters, nor any other living resident, had never seen. Between six and ten feet of water was pouring into our little city and the winds were ripping roofs off homes. Even if the floodwaters weren't coming up into a house, rain was probably falling down in it. Cameron, Louisiana, the tiny coastal town thirty minutes south of Lake Charles and right on the Gulf, was being wiped off the map as winds blew houses off their foundations. We watched in disbelief, sitting in silence as we curled up in blankets on the couch. Occasionally someone would make an innocuous comment or Dad would change the channel to see what the other station had to say about it. The constant coverage droned on, so Mom suggested Laura and I just go to bed. Staying up would do no good and not that much was going to change. It was just going to keep raining, and the news would replay the same few shots of trees bending and water rising.

As we walked to our bedroom, Mom tried to offer whatever small comfort she could. She was just as tired and scared as we were, but she was trying to keep it together for us.

"Mom, how long do you think we're going to be here?" I asked, cautiously. "I know the storm just hit, but when do you think we'll know what comes next?"

"Honestly, Katie, I don't know." I could hear the exhaustion in her voice. "I imagine your dad and I will try to go back to the city late next week to see the damage to the house and my office, but it could be a couple of weeks before the city lets people back in." She paused, took a deep breath, and began rambling. "And who knows what even happened to the schools? Even if the house is fine, if your schools are damaged, y'all can't go back. You can't just stay home all day in a city that isn't up and running. The church always floods too, so I bet there's a lot of damage there. When we get home, I bet we won't even get to go to Mass there for a while. May as well just stay here until things get back to normal."

"Our schools could be flooded? Do you think they're still there?" Laura asked quietly, tears welling up in her eyes.

Realizing she'd just unloaded all her thoughts on us, Mom pulled Laura into a hug and started rocking her on the edge of the bed.

"No, sweetie. I'm so sorry. I shouldn't have said all that. I'm sure the school is just fine, and our house too. And even if it's just a little damage, we'll be okay. Just be prepared to be here for a few weeks, okay? We may have to stay at Grandma and Papa's house for a little while, but that could be fun!"

Laura sniffled as the tears kept flowing. Mom held her close and rubbed her back. I just stood there, looking at my suitcase and backpack thrown next to the bed, my plastic container of priceless items pushed into the corner next to bins and boxes from our home. Thoughts flooded my mind as it dawned on me that this hurricane was a much bigger deal than I'd allowed myself to believe all day. Life wouldn't be back to normal for a while. No homecoming dance would be held in two weeks. I pictured the maroon dress we'd bought the week before hanging in my closet at home. I doubted I'd be competing in the speech and debate tournament the following weekend, and I certainly wasn't starting driver's ed classes in October after all.

This was unfair. And stupid. Why were my sister and I crammed into this little bedroom? Why was she crying and upset and confused, and why was my mom trying to explain away just how awful this all was? Whose fault was this? Someone, in my opinion, needed to be blamed for this mess. Someone caused this, made this storm happen and hit my hometown, and now my family was evacuated to my grandparents' house for the foreseeable future. My anger bubbled up.

"Well, this is just a load of bull . . ." I stopped short of cursing, knowing Mom would probably get mad. "Why did this thing have to hit us anyway, huh? Isn't God supposed to stop stuff like this from happening? Doesn't he love us, like even a little bit? Seems to me that if someone loves you, they wouldn't go destroying your home."

"Katie, don't talk like that." Mom quickly said. Laura's crying only intensified.

"No, Mom, I mean it. Why did this happen? Why did God do this? It isn't fair!" And I stormed out of the room.

PERFECTLY SAFE

I sheepishly apologized for my outburst the next morning, and Mom quickly forgave me. But secretly I still believed every word of what I said. There was only one explanation for a natural disaster, and it had nothing to do with water temperatures or moisture in the air. This was all God's fault, and intense frustration and hatred formed in my heart. All day I moped around the house as my parents and grandparents sat in the living room, watching the continued news coverage of the storm. Laura decided she was going to build a puzzle and dug out a thousand-piecer from the closet. Mom unpacked her latest cross-stitch project, the Knights of Columbus crest she was making for my grandfather. Dad had his laptop open, responding to emails from his boss and coworkers about what would need to be done at various bank branches. Grandma puttered in the kitchen, preparing food for an army, even though there were only six of us.

Rain poured outside as the outer bands of the hurricane moved across central Louisiana, slowly flooding the streets even three hours from the coast. All the while, we sat inside, TV on, conversation flowing, snacks at the ready. I didn't get it. We were all just hanging out, stuck in this weird limbo, unable to go home, unable to go anywhere really, and unable to make plans for the next steps. It was a waste of a Saturday, slow and sleepy and rainy, but we all seemed fine, just minding our own business and doing whatever insignificant thing could occupy our time. I spent most of my day locked in the bedroom I was sharing with Laura, reading *East of Eden*, the last book we'd been assigned in English class before evacuating. I wanted to do something normalizing and menial and act as if nothing was wrong.

But even as I tried to just read and ignore what was happening all around us, I couldn't shake my anger at God. This was all his doing, and nothing and no one was going to convince me otherwise.

Grandma cooked another delicious dinner for us that night, complete with a warm batch of chocolate chip cookies for dessert. In just forty-eight hours, we'd fallen into a routine: eat a meal, watch the news or old shows on TV Land, and go to sleep. It was becoming familiar, and I had a sneaking suspicion this was going to be my life for the next few weeks. Before we all turned in for the night, it was decided that we'd go to the nine o'clock Mass at the cathedral the next morning. Breakfast would be ready by seven thirty to give us plenty of time. When I heard the shower running at five thirty, and the TV turned on in the living room shortly after, a knot formed in my stomach. Why was someone up so early? Maybe Grandma was just restless and felt like putting the bacon on . . . but she didn't like keeping the news on, so it couldn't be her. I slipped out of bed and slinked into the living room to investigate. Dad was sitting on the couch, stuffing T-shirts, flashlights, batteries, and granola bars into a duffle bag. Mom was in the recliner, eyes fixed on the TV.

"What's going on?" I mumbled, rubbing sleep from my eyes. "Why are y'all awake?"

"Your dad has to go back to town," Mom said, eyes never breaking from the TV screen.

"Wait, what? I thought Lake Charles was empty and no one could go back? It's shut down."

"The bank called, Katie," Dad said as he continued to pack. "They need the essential personnel to come back and assess the damage of the branches and make sure things are secure in case of looters and further damage. I'm the security director. I have to go."

Silence hung in the air as I watched my dad stuff more random items into the black duffel. My mind was racing, trying to make sense of the fact that Dad was already leaving the familiar routine we'd so quickly fallen into, returning instead to a town ravaged by wind, rain, and, quite possibly, criminals. And he had no idea what he was returning to. A house? A slab? Some trees through the roof and water in the living room?

"Hey, do you think I'll need to stop and get more gas for the generator on the way back?" he casually asked Mom.

"Definitely," she said. "You could be there for a couple weeks without power."

A couple weeks? But . . . if he was going back, why weren't we going with him? I wondered. If Dad could survive for a couple weeks, then so could we.

"We'll come with you," I blurted out.

"Don't be silly, Katie," Dad said with a chuckle. "I have to go for work, and y'all need to stay here where there's power and food and not a citywide cleanup going on."

"You should eat before you go," Mom said. "I'll make you an omelet so you're full. Katie, you want anything?"

The clock sitting on the mantle began to ding, marking 5:45 a.m. "No, I'm fine," I mumbled. "Wait, Dad . . ." I said as I followed them both into the kitchen. "Dad, is it really safe to go back to Lake Charles?"

My parents looked at each other, saying more in that ten seconds of silence than they could have in ten minutes of constant chatter.

"I'll be fine, Katie," Dad said slowly. "Really. Nothing to worry about."

As if on cue, my grandfather walked in from the other room holding boxes of bullets. "Which gun did you say you're taking, Garland? Here's some ammo I had in the shed."

"You're bringing a gun?" I shouted. "But you just said it was perfectly safe to go back!"

"Katie, don't yell!" Mom fussed. "You'll wake up your sister, and we don't want to scare her."

"But if it's so safe, why are you bringing a gun? And bullets? That doesn't seem safe! Dad, you can't go!" I started to cry, angry and frustrated that this was only getting worse.

"It's just in case, Katie. I'm going to be fine, I promise. I can call from the satellite phone and let y'all know I'm all right." Dad walked over and pulled me into a hug. "And you're right . . . once everything is more settled, y'all can come help me clean up. You'll be back in Lake Charles with me sooner than you think."

"You're going back to Lake Charles? But why?" Laura stumbled into the living room, having overheard the last words my dad spoke. As Mom and Dad slowly filled Laura in on what was happening, I sat down on the couch, still confused and shocked that my nice, neat life had completely changed in just three days.

How could this be possible? How could any of this be happening? My dad was driving back to our hurricane-ravaged hometown loaded down with survival supplies while the rest of us were staying at my grandparents' house, not going back with him to whatever may be left of our home. This wasn't fair. None of this was fair.

Dad left an hour later, his giant Excursion loaded down with all the stuff he thought he'd need to stay safe and survive. We stood in the driveway, crying, sounds of our teary sniffles filled the muggy air.

"All right, girls," Mom said, as the truck rounded the corner. "We need to get ready for Mass."

"Mass?" I said. "*Mass?*" I shouted a little louder. "We're still going to *church?*"

"Of course, Katie. Where else would we go at a time like this?"

My no-nonsense mother had made up her mind. In times of tragedy, confusion, and turmoil, of course we would go to the one place where there is steady, unwavering normalcy: we would go to church to celebrate the Holy Sacrifice of the Mass.

"I'm not going," I stated. "No way. Not now. Probably not ever again. I'm not going to a place that worships a God that lets my dad drive off with bullets and a gun back into a town filled with looters and torn-up houses. God doesn't care about us. I'm not going."

"Oh, you're not, are you?" Mom stated right back. "Well, fine. That's your prerogative. I'm not going to force you to go. But just know this, Katie. You blaming God for this doesn't make it his fault. God didn't send his son to take away your pain at a moment's notice, even when it's this bad. He came here to experience that pain with you. You not going to church today doesn't prove anything other than you not really understanding that pretty basic fact."

I stood there, not caring that she was trying to teach me one of the most fundamental and important truths of the faith: that Jesus came to carry the Cross with us, not eliminate it. All I knew was this was wrong, I was hurting, and I thought Jesus didn't care about me one bit.

"I don't care, Mom. I'm not going."

"That's fine. Don't come. But we're going, because I know now more than ever that Jesus is with us in this storm, and I'm going to see him at Mass because I need him right now."

"Well, I don't," I snapped. I stomped back inside, rushed to the bedroom, and slammed the door behind me.

DO YOU EVEN CARE?

As everyone got ready for Mass, I sat defiantly on the back porch, reading my book and pouting. After everyone left, leaving me all alone with a quiet and empty space for the first time since we'd evacuated Lake Charles, I began to wander around my grandparents' tiny house, water bottle in one hand, cheese stick in the other. I didn't know what I was really looking for, but I was restless. I just needed something—anything—to look at or mess with that wasn't related to this stupid hurricane that was ruining our lives. I didn't want to keep reading *East of Eden*, nor did I just want to watch TV. I wasn't in the mood to call any of my friends, and casually surfing the Internet wouldn't be any comfort. So I wandered, opening drawers, digging through closets, searching for something to satisfy my restlessness and ease my hurt and frustration. I wandered from room to room, slipping into my grandparents' bedroom.

Sitting on my grandmother's nightstand was a small, worn book. The binding was cracked, the old black leather crumpled and the thin pages fragile after years of being turned. I'd seen it before, usually held in my grandma's wrinkled hands as she sat in her recliner, reading glasses perched on the end of her nose. A frayed ribbon stuck out from the bottom, marking the spot she'd left off.

I picked up the old Bible, perhaps the most well-used, well-loved item in the entire house. I'd never held it, I realized. I had probably never even touched it. Though I'd seen it countless times from a young age, I knew just how special and precious it was, never daring to mess with it for fear of ruining or hurting it. This was the very Word of God. It's not like my less-than-five-foot-tall grandmother would yell at me for reading the Bible, but something in me hesitated. This was her personal copy of God's divinely inspired Word—the thoughts of God in the words of men, bound together and carried around by my grandma for years. It was sacred, not just because it contained sacred scripture, but because of how precious it was to my grandmother, and how special it had been to her own mother, Gram, before her. It was much more than fifty years old, used by the matriarchs of my family as a constant recourse to the Lord.

I cautiously opened it, finding prayer cards, newspaper clippings, and small notes jotted on scraps of paper shoved between pages. The front and back inside covers were filled with passage citations written in loopy cursive. My grandmother and Gram had each created their own concordance of sorts—lists of passages in scripture that gave comfort in times of joy, confusion, loneliness, exhaustion, determination, or fear. The margins of most pages were covered with little notes, sometimes just one or two words with an arrow pointing at an underlined phrase or a bracketed section.

As I flipped through the Old and New Testaments, stories I'd known my whole life were highlighted, written around, and bookmarked. Noah built his ark and Abraham nearly killed Isaac in Genesis. Then came Moses receiving the Ten Commandments in Exodus and parting the Red Sea to lead the Israelites to freedom, followed quickly by Joshua marching around the walls of Jericho. The story of Ruth—a mere two pages—was surrounded by so many notes that it was hard to tell where scripture ended and the thoughts of my grandma and great-grandmother began. The psalms weren't much different, favorites starred and certain pages dog-eared. The pages of the gospels were so worn I could see through each one. It was evident the life of Jesus had been read and reread hundreds of times. Paul's letters were no different, the one addressed to the Ephesians covered with underlines.

As I sat on the end of the bed flipping through that little, old Bible, the story of salvation history came to life—and so too did the story of two women without whom I wouldn't be alive today. Their notes and highlights, the papers shoved inside and the pages dog-eared and torn, told the personal history of my great-grandmother and my grandma—two women with strong faith, fierce passion, and a deep love of God's Word. Looking at each page, I recognized that this Bible—and every word contained within—had been the steady constant in two lives filled with equal parts joy and sorrow. It was a vibrant and dynamic record of lives steeped in the story of God's action on earth. My grandmother's brother, Vincent, had died when he was a young man. In mourning the loss of her son, my great-grandmother had clearly read and reread the story of Lazarus being raised from the dead. Vinnie's name was written in the margins next to John 11. Matthew 17:20 was circled, a note scrawled beside it: "Small faith yields big results." I've since learned my grandmother wrote that when she had three young children and found herself juggling work and managing the home while my grandfather was in the army. She took comfort in mustard-seed-sized faith, knowing that if she believed just a little bit, God would produce a lot. John 1:41, where Andrew and John go and find Simon Peter and tell him they've found the Messiah, had one word written beside it: "Mission." Sharing about Jesus was a mission for my great-grandmother: to set forth and share with others the Anointed One, Jesus Christ.

I finally flipped open to the page marked by the thin, frayed ribbon. I'd been avoiding it, almost out of fear to know where my grandma had left off reading this book that I wasn't even sure I was allowed to be looking at. I felt as if I'd been peeking into a secret diary for the past hour, peering into the souls of my grandma and Gram. To open where grandma left off—well, that could be the ultimate invasion of her personal life. But I wanted to know: What had she been reading these past few days when we had invaded her home? There was one story bracketed on the page marked by the ribbon: Mark 4:35–41—The Calming of the Storm.

I read the story slowly, as if I'd never heard or read it before. Jesus and his disciples set out on a boat after a day of preaching to the multitudes. Tired, Jesus lies down for a nap—just a quick snooze before reaching the other side. A storm begins to rage, swelling up around them, winds and waves crashing into the boat, filling the tiny vessel with water. Terrified of sinking, the apostles frantically wake Jesus. "Master, do you care if we perish?" they shout.

I noticed the words of the apostles were underlined, an arrow drawn from them. Three words were written in the margin: "He always cares."

Jesus wakes up when the apostles cry out. He stands up, raises his arms, and calms the storm with the words, "Peace, be still." Those words were circled, another arrow drawn from them. The note in the margin read, "He brings peace."

At these words of Jesus, the winds cease, the waves quiet down, and calm rests on the violent and turbulent waters. Jesus turns to the apostles and questions them: "Why are you so fearful? How is it that you have no faith?" Another arrow. Another note, reading, "Have faith in the storm."

I sat there holding the Bible, open to this passage, for I don't even know how long. Long enough for my feet to fall asleep and my back to hurt from hunching over. Those few verses—this story I'd heard and read and knew from all my years of Catholic school and Mass attendance—was entirely new, fresh, and relevant as I sat in my grandparent's bedroom in late September of 2005.

There I was, sitting in a boat being furiously tossed about in a storm. And where was Jesus? Taking a nap. I was a faithless follower, terrified and worried about what was right in front of my face: big waves, loud thunder, and fierce winds. I was a broken-down believer, crying out to Jesus, "Do you even care if I perish?" as I watched everything I knew and held precious potentially slip away before my eyes. Did Jesus even care? Was he even paying attention? Or was he sleeping, literally napping on the job, ignoring me in my desperation and hurt?

The personal notes of my grandmother and great-grandmother showed me they too must've felt the same way at some point. They'd underlined the question shouted by those beleaguered and terrified apostles, and they'd processed and prayed with that moment, concluding that yes, Jesus always cares, whether we realize it or not. They had learned, as I would too, that Jesus can stand in the midst of that storm, raise his arms, and control the chaos that seems to be winning the day. Jesus brings peace. This is who he is: the peacemaker, the one who naps but always wakes when we call upon him. Tears began to well up in my eyes as I sat there with the Bible, further contemplating what was happening in the story and what was happening in my life.

The last note written in the margin gave me pause. Jesus asks the apostles why they're lacking in faith. Clearly they know who he is and what he's capable of, and yet they frantically wake him up to stop a simple storm that didn't seem to be that big of a deal to Jesus but was of great concern for them. My grandmother, in her reading of the story, had written, "Have faith in the storm" off to the side.

I didn't get it. Have faith in *Jesus* during the storm? Or, have faith in the storm itself? Which was it? How had Grandma and Gram read this passage? How should I? Was I meant to trust in the actual storm, having faith that perhaps the turbulence, chaos, and unknown would lead me to something greater—perhaps deeper faith? Or was I supposed to have faith and trust in Jesus during the storm, believing in his sovereign power and might in the midst of that turbulence and chaos? Or was it both?

I read and reread the story, each word taking on life and meaning as it sounded in my head. I read it aloud, and then I read it silently to myself. I kept looking at the notes in the margins, gleaning meaning from the interpretations of my family's matriarchs. The yellowed pages and small black print began to blur as I continued to stare at the page, but I couldn't look away.

I was in the storm myself, no longer just reading this story but sitting in the boat upon the sea, being tossed about. Jesus was asleep on the job while I nearly drowned, and I was trying to wake him up. And very clearly, Jesus was looking me square in the eye and asking me why I had such little faith. Did I not trust him? Was I not aware of all that he could do? Or was I so blinded by what was right in front of me that I ignored all that I knew to be true and had believed for so long?

The phone rang, snapping me back to reality. I jumped, the Bible nearly falling from my hands. I grabbed the phone quickly. "Hello?" I said cautiously. This was my grandparent's house, after all. I had no idea who could be calling at almost ten o'clock on a Sunday morning.

"Katie, is that you?" It was Dad. "You didn't go to church?"

"Dad!" I shouted. "No . . . I didn't go to church. Where are you? Are you back home? What's going on? How is it?"

"I made it, yes. I'm back in Lake Charles. No traffic. No one is headed that way because you can't get into the city without credentials. Are they not home from Mass yet?"

"No. It's just me. So you got in, right? How's the house? Is it still there? What's it like?" I peppered him with questions and he started laughing. "It's not funny, Dad. What's going on?"

"Katie . . . calm down. I wanted to tell your mother first." A long pause followed and I mentally prepared myself for the worst. The house was gone, I knew it. Blew right off the nine-foot posts, trees through the windows, roof caved in. Our entire life was gone. It had to be. Dad wouldn't be hesitating for so long if he had good news.

"Katie . . . Holly Hill Road is pretty torn up. The Strouds [our neighbor to the right] have a tree on their deck. The Reons [neighbors to the left] flooded. The house will have to be totally gutted. CNN is reporting from the other end of the street because all the power lines are down."

"Dad . . ." I said quietly, "what about our house?"

"Katie, you're never going to believe this."

I held my breath.

"Guess what's still sitting on our front porch?"

"We have a front porch?" I shouted into the phone.

"Oh, yeah, we have a front porch. And a back porch. And an entire house! Katie, my shoes didn't move. Those nasty boat shoes your mom hates . . . they're still there! It's like it didn't even rain. There are branches down and the yard is a wreck, but the house is fine. Katie, the basketball hoop just toppled over. It got stuck in the mud! Didn't even float away!"

I started laughing, barely able to contain my excitement and relief. I couldn't believe it. The house was fine. Our home wasn't gone. Dad needed to hurry and get to bank headquarters to begin assessing the property damage there, so we hung up after our few minutes of rejoicing. I collapsed back onto the bed, a colossal weight lifted off my shoulders. A pain in my chest that I hadn't even realized had been there for the past few days was gone. There, open beside me, was the Gospel of Mark, the calming of the storm still bracketed, the notes still jumping off the page.

"His shoes didn't even move . . ." I whispered to myself, shaking my head in utter disbelief as I stared down at the open Bible. "His shoes didn't even move . . ."

I guess I needed to have faith in the storm after all.

ACCESS POINT

The next few weeks ticked by slowly, our evacuation routine becoming more solidified and regular with each passing day. Sharing a room with my little sister and watching the same TV shows day after day were getting annoying. Against all odds, we were getting tired of my grandma's cooking. We knew we'd probably have an extended school year, possibly losing some of our summer break, and Mom was becoming increasingly frustrated with her inability to get back to work. We all wanted life to return to normal as soon as possible, but at the end of the day, our house was fine and we were grateful.

My attitude slowly shifted as I began to realize that the damage from a storm, in whatever form it came, was no match for the immense power of Jesus Christ. In fact, even our friends back home who had suffered great losses—destroyed roofs, flooded houses, lost property—were keeping a positive and faithful outlook. It was as if we all knew that the storm, as strong as it had been, was not caused by Jesus, but was certainly calmed by him. In fact, Jesus was with us in the storm, manifesting his power to us in the midst of crashing waves and tumultuous waters. When I read Mark 4 and saw the notes and thoughts written in the margins, I had begun to understand that Jesus' abiding presence and unwavering power are great, something to be trusted and counted on. For me, the words of scripture had brought me back to the understanding that the abiding, abundant presence of the Word made Flesh, who loves and knows me far better than I ever truly realized, would never leave and his power would never cease to be.

My whole life, the calming of the storm in the Gospel of Mark had been just a nice story tucked away in scripture, read a few times a year at Mass and depicted in the occasional piece of Christian art. In fact, scripture was no longer just this collection of familiar stories with stunning and confusing moments to me. It began to dawn on me that the Bible wasn't meant to be just a mixture of random snapshots telling the tales of people throughout the course of human history.

Each passage, each story, was a moment capturing the action of God in time. The words of scripture, inspired by the Holy Spirit and written down by selected individuals, now bound together and held in my hands, weren't tales of "how to live a good life" or a list of "do this or don't do that." The words of sacred scripture capture the very Word itself. Each moment, story, phrase, line, miracle, parable, genealogy, parable, poem, song, and historical narrative is an invitation to encounter Jesus himself. When I met him there, in those stories and on those pages, it became evident that Jesus sees and knows me, far more clearly than I ever realized. Scripture is an access point to Jesus, telling us the story of who he is and what he has done so we can come to love him. The stories of the people who waited for him, walked with him, and proclaimed him allow us to approach Jesus, coming to know him intimately and living differently as a result of that encounter.

Far too often, we think of the Bible as either a paperweight meant to collect dust on coffee tables and bookshelves, sitting there only to prove to household visitors that Jesus matters, just a little bit, in our lives. We may relegate scripture to the status of a rule book, letting it place ridiculous demands upon our lives, using it only as a measure of what we've done right or wrong. But scripture is so much more. It is the very story of who God is and, because we belong to him, who we are. It is the great story made up of many small stories that instructs us how we are to live and abide in his love. When we read the Bible, we come to know and love Jesus and learn how to live for him. It is a beautiful and essential access point for meeting Jesus.

In prayer, we lift our hearts to the Lord, crying out from the depths of our being in adoration and praise, petitioning his merciful and generous heart, and thanking him for the abundant gifts he has already provided. Our lifted hearts beg the Lord to reveal all that he is so we can become all we are meant to be, in him. We grow close to the Lord when we pray. Our hearts soften as we lift them up. We are formed more fully in his image when we intimately speak to him, and we long to hear his still small voice in the quiet of our hearts. When we pick up our Bible, whether tattered and well used or brand new and unopened, we quiet that voice that we have raised in prayer and open our hearts and minds to listen for what he has to say.

The inspired words of the Bible lead us to Jesus, the Word made Flesh. And when we meet Jesus—when we truly encounter him in the pages of scripture and come to know him—our lives take on a whole new meaning. Our dry bones come to life. We come to live and move and have our being as we read these words, because we are meeting Christ Jesus.

When we approach the pages of our Bible with the mind-set that this text is life-giving and leads us to Jesus himself, then each line takes on new meaning and brings us into this new, enriched life, centered and focused on him. We begin to see it as the living Word, breathing life into our relationship with Jesus. The note-filled Bible I found in my grandparents' bedroom was proof that at least two people in my family knew what scripture truly is—the Word of God, spoken intimately and directly to each and every one of us. The stories from the gospels, the moments in the Acts of the Apostles, and the lessons in the epistles aren't just mere historical events or collected facts. This is Jesus' life, shared with us so we can see that he perfectly understands all that we experience in our own lives because he lived among us.

The scriptures are meant to touch the very depths of our souls as we seek Jesus and desire relationship with him. Opening the Bible and reading the first book, Genesis, helps us realize that the creation story is meant for us. God made something from nothing, and spoke being into existence, purely out of love. He did it for you; he did it for me. We're in the Garden of Eden, reaching out to take what we shouldn't simply because we selfishly want it. We're Cain, jealous of what others offer to the Lord. We're Abraham, fearful of the unknown, and we're Sarah, laughing when God's promises seem impossible. We're Moses, hesitating to go back to the places we've left, and we're Joshua, bravely walking into the land promised to us. We're Ruth, committed in faith, and Esther, courageous in the face of evil. We are Job, struggling to see joy in the midst of suffering and hurt, but constant in faith. We're David asking forgiveness, Solomon begging for wisdom, and Josiah restoring order. We are Tobit wandering the desert, Daniel facing lions, and Jeremiah hesitant to step up and serve. We are Matthew, minding our own business when Jesus calls us to follow him. We're Peter, encouraged to throw our nets onto the other side of the boat to bring in a fruitful catch. We're the woman sitting at the well, seen and loved even in our sinfulness and shame. We're Mary standing at the foot of the Cross, Thomas doubting when we can't see something explicitly, and even sometimes Judas, betraying our Lord and selling out for something quick and easy. We're Paul, totally changed by an unexpected encounter with Jesus. We're Stephen, standing up for our faith, even to the point of a painful death. We're John, shown incredible things that we barely understand.

When we read the Bible, we are looking at more than collections of stories and familiar sayings: each word is leading us closer to the Word. Jesus is there, in those words, showing us who he is and how loved we are by him. It's in those pages that Jesus' very real and tangible life on this earth is revealed to us. We see Jesus weep and we know that he felt sadness and sorrow. When we discover that Jesus became annoyed and frustrated, flipping over tables to prove his point, then we know that he, like us, got angry. The Bible places us before Jesus and we more clearly understand just exactly who he is: the God who experienced the whole range of human emotions, walked upon physical ground, laid his head down to sleep, laughed with his friends, and wept for his enemies. We come to see that meeting Jesus isn't all that different than meeting a friend in kindergarten for the first time: there's something in common between us and Jesus. I discover that when I read the Bible and I think you will too.

Our project is to get to know Jesus and walk the journey of life with him, experiencing the greatest and most fruitful adventure we'll ever know. We can never exhaust all that he is or fully grasp the great depths of his love for us. The Bible is an invaluable guide to aid us on that journey.

DEVELOP A HABIT OF READING SCRIPTURE

As prayer is so much more than a chore that places tedious demands on us, reading, studying, and contemplating scripture is not engagement with a random collection of stories and short verses that you're either confused by or meant to memorize. While you may be required to read the Bible as part of school or parish program, no one can compel you to do more than that. But the Spirit will certainly urge you to do so. And if you want to know and follow Jesus, well, then, you will need to. Think of the Bible less as textbook and more as guidebook for the journey that is your life. Each story and phrase, each parable and teaching, and every single person introduced is meant to deeply reveal God's divine plan and how we fit into it.

Even still, the Bible can be intimidating. The Bible is unwieldy; most editions of this most popular book of all time are well over a thousand pages long. The font is often tiny, crossing at least four columns over each two-page spread. The footnotes are usually even smaller! Unless you're a scholar, or have put handy-dandy tabs on the side, it can take a while to find what you're looking for. The unfamiliar names, funny words, and sometimes confusing scenarios don't necessarily make God's divinely inspired Word easy reading. Of all the books you have picked up, I'm guessing the Bible hasn't often—or ever—been your first choice. But we can't let those incidental and random realities deter us from diving in. We really must choose to dive in, trusting that in each moment, phrase, and passage is a chance to encounter Jesus, who will meet us in whatever condition we happen to be.

So don't just pick up the Bible and start from page one, planning to make it all the way to the end in a month. Some people try that, and most end up discouraged. It's far easier, and more fruitful, to take it piece by piece, section by section, and give yourself ample time to really understand why certain books are the way they are. You'll come to see why Genesis is first, how the psalms progressively build, why the gospels seem to repeat each other, and why Paul's letters are at the end. It would be foolish to just randomly sign up to run a marathon without having done, at the very least, a few 5K runs to train yourself in endurance, speed, stamina, and style. So why do we just randomly approach scripture, assuming we can read it all at once, without putting in the time, effort, and attention to understanding what we're approaching and who we are meeting?

You'll need a copy of the Bible to do this, of course, and it's probably best to get your own that you can take notes in, carry around with you, and have at the ready. Don't just use a decorative copy sitting on a coffee table (or the free copy found in a hotel room). Invest in one that you can use regularly and grow with day by day. The two best translations to turn to are the New American Bible, Revised Edition, (an earlier edition of this translation is what we hear at Mass and other liturgies) or the New Revised Standard Version Bible, Catholic Edition (what most theologians and professors use in academic studies). Either translation is solid, accessible, and will provide exactly what you need to get started. Some Bibles come with great, detailed comments and extra articles throughout. Look into using the Ignatius Study Bible, the Catholic Youth Bible, or the Didache Bible if you want a Bible that helps you study the text in depth.

Some Bibles are more basic, simple printings with just footnotes on the bottom of the pages and no extra commentaries. These footnotes give very basic insights into the meanings of words, the context of certain passages, other verses that are similar, and where to find more information. These are simple, helpful notes to guide you in making sense of what you're reading.

You can also make use of external commentaries that give insight into specific books. One of the most thorough commentaries available is the *Navarre Bible Commentary*, which goes book by book through the Bible and gives remarkably detailed information. Dr. Peter Kreeft, a professor at Boston College, has a great book: *You Can Understand the Bible: A Practical and Illuminating Guide into Each Book of the Bible*. He provides straightforward insights into each book of the Bible without being overly complicated or confusing. Lastly, when things in scripture are confusing, seem contradictory, or make you curious, seek wisdom and insight from people you know have studied the Bible and know their faith, such as your youth minister, a theology teacher, or your parish priest. Sometimes in-person conversation is the best way to make sense of certain passages, leading you ever closer to an encounter with Jesus in the Word of God.

Start with the Old Testament, and specifically the first five books of the Bible, known as the Pentateuch or the Torah. For our Jewish brothers and sisters, these are the five most sacred books of scripture, because they tell the beautiful and amazing story of God's creative action and his calling forth of the Chosen People, the Israelites. The stories are probably familiar to you. You've sung songs about them at Vacation Bible School, colored the pictures, heard them proclaimed at Mass, or read them on your own. As with everything in the Bible, though, it's also worth taking another look, trying to discover how a passage can take on new meaning for you at various times throughout your life. Sometimes you can totally relate to Abraham laughing at

God's promises and at other times you relate to Abraham willing to sacrifice everything to show his faith. He's the same Abraham, but we encounter him and get to know him at different stages on his own adventure with the Lord. So too with us—we can return to the familiar stories of the Bible to see where we are on our journey toward Jesus and learn how to walk with him more closely.

As you read the scripture passages I list later in this chapter, don't hesitate to read further. It's very easy for the story or passage to spur a desire to keep reading. That's one of the most beautiful things about diving into the Word: you'll want to go further, read more, and look at the bigger picture. It's great to start with these isolated bits and pieces to help establish a habit of reading scripture regularly, but don't be afraid to just keep going. If you read one suggested passage a day from the twelve Old Testament books I list later in this chapter and follow my instructions for the book of Job, it'll take you just under eight weeks to make your way through this smattering of the Old Testament. That's only two months to build the habit of reading the Word and let it wash over you so that you can further come to know and love Jesus. Take the simple questions I offer as kickstarters to help you approach the texts less as a passive spectator and more as an engaged learner. I find journaling or jotting down notes in the margins (as my grandmother and great-grandmother did) help me get more involved with the text.

FIRST STEPS

Each passage I suggest below carries its own unique meaning and a particular pride of place in the Bible. This isn't an exhaustive reading of the depth, nuances, context, or history of the stories listed. Rather, think of these assigned passages as appetizers: let these words inspire you to *keep* reading and discovering and understanding the beautiful story of our salvation that the scriptures reveal to us. Allow yourself to be fully immersed in the text, getting lost in the words so you can be found in the Lord.

From Genesis

- Genesis 1 and 2: The Creation Stories
  - → God made something from nothing, out of love, for you. What have you created in your own life? Why were you proud of what you had done/made?

- Genesis 3: The Fall
  - → Have you ever directly disobeyed someone, say, a parent or teacher? Why? And what happened as a result?

- Genesis 4: Cain and Abel
  - → What do you offer the Lord? Is it your best?
  - → Have you ever been envious of others' gifts?

- Genesis 7–9: Noah and the Ark
  - → If God were to call you to do something radical, would you have the faith to say yes and do it?

- Genesis 12: The Call of Abram
  - → What do you want most from God? Abram wanted a son. God instead told him to move to a new land first, and he went. Have you expressed your desires to the Lord? Would you get up and go where he told you to go?

- Genesis 15: The Covenant with Abram
  - → God asks Abram to look at the stars and trust him. What kind of trust do you have in God and his promises? Rate that trust on a scale of 1 to 10. What do you need to give over to him so you can trust him more?

- Genesis 22: The Testing of Abraham
  - → What do you need to sacrifice in your life? Think of something practical that the Lord may be asking you to give up to show him your devotion and love.

- Genesis 27: Jacob Deceives His Father
    - → Have you ever lusted after something? Have you been so jealous that you would do anything to get your way? How did you feel after you acted on that jealousy?

- Genesis 37: Joseph Sold into Slavery in Egypt
    - → Think of a time when people you loved and trusted betrayed you. What did that feel like?

- Genesis 45: Joseph Forgives His Brothers
    - → Who do you need to forgive for betraying, hurting, or angering you? What grudge is deeply embedded in your heart, keeping you from Jesus?

Exodus

- Exodus 2:23–3:22: The Call of Moses
    - → How do you think you would respond if you stumbled upon a burning bush? Would you have immediately gone to Egypt and done as God commanded? Have there been any moments in your life when you knew for certain God was telling you to do something? How did you respond?

- Exodus 12: The Passover
    - → What stands out most when you read the Passover ritual? What sounds familiar? What's confusing?

- Exodus 14 and 15: The Parting of the Red Sea
    - → When in your life have you experienced the Lord delivering you to safety? How have you thanked him?

- Exodus 20: The Ten Commandments
    - → Which commandments do you most struggle to follow? Why?

- Exodus 32: The Golden Calf
    - → Why do you think the people worshiped the calf? Have you ever doubted God's plans in your life? How have you acted as a result of that doubt?

Deuteronomy

- Deuteronomy 1: The Twelve Scouts
  - → Why were the scouts scared of what they saw in Canaan? What makes it difficult to trust the unseen plans of God?

- Deuteronomy 6: The Great Commandment
  - → Do you think you follow this law in your life? Why or why not? What changes do you need to make to love the Lord more?

- Deuteronomy 30: The Choice between Life and Death
  - → With life and death set before you, which do you choose? How can you turn your heart more fully to the Lord God?

- Deuteronomy 32: The Song of Moses
  - → How would you thank the Lord for all he has done for you? What stories would you tell, from your own life, that show how the Lord has acted?

Joshua

- Joshua 1: The Promises of Assistance
  - → Do you believe that the Lord God is with you wherever you go? If so, why? If not, then why?

- Joshua 24: Reminder of Divine Goodness
  - → How does this chapter help you recall all that God has done so far for the Israelite people? Where do you fit into this story?

Ruth

- Ruth 1: Naomi and Ruth
  - → Why do you think Ruth stayed with Naomi? Who in your life do you think you'd do this for? Why?

1 Samuel

- 1 Samuel 1: Hannah's Prayer
  - → Have you ever desired something so much that you prayed as fervently as Hannah did for a son?

- 1 Samuel 2:1–10: Hannah's Offering to God
  - → What line stands out most to you in this prayer Hannah says? Why?

- 1 Samuel 3: The Call of Samuel
  - → What would you do if the Lord called you to a life of service for him? How would you respond to the moment of hearing God's voice?

- 1 Samuel 8: The Demand for a King
  - → Why do the Israelite people want a king? What has God granted you, in your life, that you have accepted cautiously or with pause?

- 1 Samuel 16–17: David Is Called Forth
  - → What is unique and special about David? What qualities of his would you like to see in your own life?
  - → What are some giants that you need to defeat? What can you do to take them down?

- 1 Samuel 24: David Spares Saul
  - → When have you forgiven someone or shown mercy to them? What was that experience like? When have you been forgiven or been shown mercy?

2 Samuel

- 2 Samuel 8: David's Prayer
  - → What lengths would you go to in order to ensure the Lord is properly worshiped in your life?

- 2 Samuel 11: David's Sin
  - → Why is it such a big deal that David sinned as he did? What sin have you committed recently that upsets you, causes you shame, and from which you'd like to repent? Why?

- 2 Samuel 22:1–23:7: David's Prayer and Last Words
  - → Choose four or five phrases from these prayers that stick out to you as words that you could say in your life, right now.

Esther

- Esther 4: The Prayers of Mordecai and Esther
  - → How do these prayers speak to your heart? What are they saying that you would say to the Lord yourself? What have you not said but perhaps want to?

Job

- Read three chapters of Job each day until you have made your way through the entire book (it will take two weeks). Each day, ask yourself these three questions:
  - → How do I respond to suffering in my own life?
  - → How is Job an example to me?
  - → What do I need to do to respond to the trials in my life?

Isaiah

- Isaiah 9: Praise to God
  - → Of the titles given to Jesus (who is prophesied in these verses), which one do you most relate to? Which one gives you most comfort, encouragement, and strengthens your own faith?

- Isaiah 25: Encouragement
  - → How do these words of Isaiah encourage you? What has the Lord saved you from? What do you need him to continue to do in your life?

- Isaiah 42: The Servant of the Lord
    - → Who is being described in these verses? How has Jesus done these things in your life?

Jeremiah

- Jeremiah 1: The Call of Jeremiah
    - → Have you ever been scared to respond to the Lord's call? Why or why not?
    - → What scares you most about living a life of faith and relationship with Jesus?

- Jeremiah 17:5–13: True Wisdom
    - → Who is blessed? Who is faithful? What does the Lord alone do in your life?

- Jeremiah 20: Jeremiah's Interior Crisis
    - → When have you felt tricked or betrayed? Have you ever felt that way about God?
    - → Have you ever felt abandoned by Jesus? What was that like?

Daniel

- Daniel 3: The Fiery Furnace
    - → When have you been tested in your faith? Did you stand up for what you believe? Do you think you'd have accepted death in a fire to proclaim your belief in the one, true God?
    - → Look at the long list of "Bless the Lord" phrases and choose two or three that stand out to you. Why do they stand out? What about the lines you chose speaks to your heart?

- Daniel 6: The Lion's Den
    - → Why is Daniel thrown into the lion's den? What is admirable about his faith and devotion?

THE BIBLE'S PRAYER BOOK

The book of Psalms holds a sort of pride of place in the Bible. Not only is it smack-dab in the middle, but Psalms doesn't tell a story, introduce characters, or narrate historical moments. Instead, the psalms are heartfelt personal prayers used for worship. They were written for liturgical services, meant to give glory and praise to God. The psalms weren't spoken; they were sung. These are hymns of praise, lament, petition, adoration, confession, and thanksgiving. Sound familiar? These are, in a real way, spontaneous prayers that were written down. The psalms are a wonderful gift to us if we find ourselves stuck when we try to spontaneously pray ourselves, or when we try to enter into a time of meditation or rest in the Lord. They can serve as starting points, helping us dive deeper into the depths of our own hearts as we dig into the words.

There are 150 psalms in total, each one unique. Some, such as Psalm 4, are beautiful reflections on the need to completely trust the Lord. Others, such as the very next one, Psalm 5, are desperate pleas for assistance and help. Some are very familiar, such as Psalm 23, which begins, "The LORD is my shepherd" and has been depicted in many works of art for centuries, reminding us that Jesus the Good Shepherd watches over us, even through the darkest times of life. Other psalms are lesser known, more obscure, heard only from time to time at Mass, such as Psalm 48, a reflection on God's kingdom and how we are meant to ponder his steadfast love in our worship.

Approaching the psalms can be just as intimidating as approaching the entire Bible. There are a lot of words crammed into 150 sections, and there's no end in sight when it comes to unpacking their meaning. One of the best (and easiest) ways to begin diving into the psalms is to read just one per day, once in the morning, again around midday, and then right before you go to bed at night. Let the psalm you read that day be the guiding force to your steps. Return to it, thinking about each line and asking yourself how those words are applicable to your life in that specific moment. While you are likely not walking into war against your enemies, as was King David and his army, you do face daily struggles. The psalms can help you build your confidence in God's actions rather than depending so greatly on your own power.

You certainly have plenty to thank the Lord for, and you definitely have a longing within your heart to know him more fully. We are all called to give praise for a lifetime. The psalms are a perfect way to do that; let these sacred words become your own. Your ears are opened in reading scripture, lifting your heart further.

Don't become overwhelmed by the great number of psalms. Just start with Psalm 1 and work your way through to Psalm 150. That's about five months of consistent, daily reading of the Bible's prayer book. If you're feeling ambitious, or have really fallen in love with reading scripture, then read and ponder a daily psalm along with another passage (perhaps something from the New Testament). This will, at the very least, get you in the habit of using the psalms as a beautiful aid to your personal prayer and help you further grow to know Jesus. The psalms were part of the Jewish catalog of prayers, so it's entirely reasonable to believe that Jesus would have prayed some of these psalms himself. He would have said things such as, "Shout joyfully to God, all the earth" (Ps 66:2), or "My God, my God, why have you abandoned me?" (Ps 22:2). You are drawing closer to the Word made Flesh when you hold these 150 psalms close and let them penetrate your heart and mind.

FRESH EYES ON THE GOSPELS

A few years ago, while in the midst of juggling a busy work schedule, traveling extensively to various youth ministry events, and attempting to maintain a social life, I noticed that my relationship with Jesus was kind of taking a back seat. Prayer, Mass, and even just thinking about Jesus outside of work wasn't much of a priority, and I wanted to hit a reset button. So I did what I love to do: found a good book about Jesus and decided to read it. I found a simple, straightforward book, *Theology for Beginners*, written by an Englishman named Frank Sheed. It was designed to give the reader basic theological explanations of complicated topics, such as the Doctrine of the Trinity, the Church's understanding of the Eucharist, and what happens when we die. While I didn't necessarily consider myself a theological beginner (though we all are, at the end of the day), I figured it would be a nice addition to my library and maybe help me get back on track. I didn't get very far in the book. Not because I didn't like it, but because within a few chapters Sheed placed a challenge to his readers that forced me to go pick up my Bible.

Less than a third of the way through *Theology for Beginners*, Sheed quotes G. K. Chesterton, another Englishman who inspired millions with his writings, speeches, and virtuous life. Sheed was writing about sacred scripture: why it matters, where it comes from, and how we should approach it. He referenced Chesterton, saying "We have to read the gospels as if we are seeing and hearing them for the first time." I thought it was an interesting concept—to act as if every gospel story and moment, from the birth of Jesus to his Resurrection and Ascension, was entirely fresh and new. This would require reading the long, sometimes tedious gospels as if I had never read them before, as if these familiar moments weren't just boring repetitive stories but were actually amazing and miraculous, as they should be!

How many times have you been in Mass, stood up for the proclamation of the Gospel, and immediately tuned out the moment you realized what story was being read? You've heard the Parable of the Prodigal Son dozens of times. You know that Jesus turned water into wine at Cana. You certainly remember that Judas betrayed Jesus for thirty pieces of silver and that Peter denied him three times. The gospels aren't new, but he who is directly presented to us in the gospels—Jesus Christ, Word made Flesh dwelling among us—is always new. The gospels, which are not new, contain accounts of the life, teachings, miracles, and witness of he who never gets old. So we can't approach them with our "same ole, same ole" attitude that causes us to forget just how beautiful and incredible Jesus' time on earth was and what it means for us today.

I took up this challenge from Frank Sheed and G. K. Chesterton. I decided to read the gospels with fresh eyes. I wanted to meet Jesus for the first time, as if I didn't know what was going to happen next. Does he raise Lazarus from the dead? Well . . . I'll have to keep reading to find out! Will he feed the crowd of five thousand people? Who knows! What's he going to say to all those dirty moneychangers in the Temple? Spoiler alert . . . he's going to flip over their tables and crack the whip. I wasn't trying to read the gospels as someone ignorant of the story of Jesus. Instead, I wanted to read them as someone who could still be surprised, wowed, and grateful for all that Jesus said, did, and continues to do and say in my life.

I can't stress enough how valuable this approach to the gospels was for me. I began with the Gospel of Matthew and read two or three chapters every day, whenever I had the chance. I didn't stop until I finished the Gospel of John. Each chapter, whether a miracle story, a teaching narrative, a personal encounter with someone, or a parable, helped shed light on Jesus as both God and man. It wasn't easy to just turn off the "I've heard this before" switch or eliminate my preconceived notions of who Jesus is and what he did. But that was precisely the challenge: to dive into the story with the attitude of "What could this mean for me right now?" or "How would I have reacted in this situation or scenario?" The four central books of scripture became a foundation for my daily life. Try doing this yourself. Begin reading the gospels with fresh eyes, as if you've never heard any of it before. Start with Matthew, and work your way through with two or three chapters a day. Let the familiar words take on new life as you try to keep an open mind to the new things that may jump out and touch your heart.

LECTIO DIVINA

As cheesy as it may sound, the Bible is a love letter. It's God speaking to us, revealing himself to us, in words written down to tell the story of how he has acted over the course of human history. We read those words not just so we have a collective memory of all that God *used* to do, but so that we can engage with the reality of what God is still doing today. When we read scripture, we're not simply trying to comprehend some concepts or story. We're reading to remember, to actively engage, and to let these moments come to life in our lives.

Lectio divina, Latin for "holy reading" or "divine reading," is an ancient and beautiful practice of reading the scriptures in a prayerful, contemplative way. Each passage or section suggested so far can (and probably should) be read using lectio divina, because then you'll be looking at the text less as something static and more as something living, which will allow you to engage with it on a deeply personal and life-changing level.

There are four steps to lectio divina, and each step builds upon the one before it, leading you deeper into the text. It's often easiest to become well versed in the practice of lectio divina by turning to narrative passages of the Bible—stories, parables, specific moments where Jesus teaches or heals someone. These narrative passages allow you to become immersed in a place and time, with people and dialogue. Tactile stories help you dive more fully into the text and follow through the four steps of lectio divina, aiding you as you build the muscle of reading the Bible well. We're not all called to be contemplatives who spend hours and hours each day reading the Bible. At the very least, though, we can and should take a significant chunk of time each day to move through these four steps and immerse ourselves in God's Word.

Step 1: Reading (Lectio)

The first step of lectio divina requires actually reading the passage. It's best to do this aloud, listening to the words as you read them. Don't just gloss over them quickly. Be intentional with each phrase as you say and hear it. Read the passage a second time, slower, still aloud. Repeat this, three or four times, reading the words at a slower pace each time.

Pay attention to the details of the passage as you are reading. Picture where the event is taking place, or try to associate images with the words if there's not a specific location or setting. This first step makes use of your senses. You are reading the words with your eyes, speaking them with your voice, hearing them with your ears, and then trying to visualize the physical context. What could you touch in the story? What could you taste? Maybe you're at the Last Supper . . . what does the room smell like? Feel the rough wood of the table underneath your hands. Allow yourself to be fully immersed in the atmosphere of the passage. This will make the text come to life.

Place yourself into the scene. Where are you standing? Who are you in the story? Are you Peter, denying Jesus? Or are you one of the people asking him if he knows Jesus? Are you an innocent bystander who witnesses Jesus heal the blind man, or are you Bartimaeus yourself, crying out for aid? In this first step, you are trying to fully enter into the story so that your mind can run wild and picture and experience everything that is happening. You're tapping into your imagination so the text comes to life.

Step 2: Meditate/Think (Meditatio)

Now it's time to move beyond experiencing the words in a somewhat physical way and let the words begin to lead you closer to the presence of God. How do these words affect your life in this moment? You are being invited to respond *to* the words. You're pondering them, asking, "What does this Word mean for me at this time, right now?" or "What would I do in this scenario then, or now?" It's not just looking inward. You are not meditating on the words of scripture in a self-centered way. You are trying to let the text move beyond being a nice story or message and instead become deeply personal for you.

You've imagined the scene, noticed the details, and put yourself into the story or passage. Now *be* in that story. Think it through, really ponder each word from each line at each moment. These aren't isolated, ancient events, but very relevant, very present moments where the Lord is reaching into your heart and mind, wanting to meet you. In a very practical sense, when you spend time on this step, work through the following questions:

- Where are you in the story? Who are you? Think back to all the physical things you pictured during the first step and go deeper with your imagination. It may be helpful to close your eyes. Make sure you're in a space that isn't filled with distractions such as your phone, computer, television, or even other people. Let your senses be overwhelmed by scripture, not stuff that's physically around you.

- How does this event, moment, line, or story make you feel? Are you nervous, scared, or frightened? Are you confident, encouraged, enlightened, or excited? Are you empowered? Or are you perhaps a bit held back by what is being shared and explained?
- Based on what you are seeing in yourself as you think about this passage, what do you need to change in order for these words to take on flesh in your own life? In other words, what will be different and how will you be different as a result of reading this passage?
- What can you learn most from this passage? What do you think God is trying to say to you as you read these words?

Step 3: Pray (Oratio)

You've read the story or passage, you've thought intensely about what it means, and now you have something to say in response. Now is the time to actively lift up your heart and speak to the Lord about what you heard. You pray, talking to God in a spontaneous, honest way. You're responding to what you've read and thought about, sharing what has hit your heart, what has awakened your senses, and what has lodged in your mind. Ask yourself these questions:

- What do I want to say to God about these words? What do I need him to hear?
- What am I longing for after reading these words? What do I want from him? How do I want to grow or go deeper?
- What can I say to God right now that maybe I've been hiding? Am I upset? Am I joyful? Is there grief or sadness, anger or frustration, deep within me? Am I grateful for blessings given? Am I in need of help or aid?

- How can I tell the Lord that I am ready to accept his will? What can I say to show him that I am allowing these words to guide me in a deeper way?

Step 4: Contemplate (Contemplatio)

You've done a lot throughout these first three steps: read, thought, and then prayed. Now it's time to sit back and let the Lord talk to you again. This fourth and final step is the listening step. It's the passive movement of lectio divina because you simply receive God's response to all that you have thought about and then said to him. It's not like you can just say, "Okay, Jesus, you may talk to me now" and wait to hear that still, small voice. Instead (and yes, this is tough), you simply open your heart and mind to resting in God's presence and enjoying his love.

Yes, I know that sounds super abstract and maybe even impossible. You're just supposed to sit there and receive something from God? You may wonder how to know if you're doing it correctly. Think of it like this: You've been looking at God by reading these words, placing yourself into the passage, and then speaking to him from your heart. Now it's time to let God look back at you, and for you to let yourself be seen. This is challenging because it requires surrender. It demands that you don't "do" anything except simply "be"—and that isn't easy. Don't be discouraged if you feel like maybe you're doing it wrong. Again, contemplation is something happening to you, not something you are accomplishing on your own. You are entering into the mystery of the Word so that you can allow the Word to speak to your heart and love you for all that you are. St. Teresa of Avila describes it like this: "Contemplative prayer is nothing else than a close sharing between friends; it means taking time frequently to be alone with him who we know loves us."

When you enter into this step, it's helpful to close your eyes, take a few deep breaths, and maybe repeat the phrase "Lord Jesus, I'm open" a few times, very softly.

DON'T BE IGNORANT

In the fourth century, a man was born in modern-day Slovenia. Remarkably, this man affects you at this very moment. His name was Jerome. After living a bit of the party life for years, he converted to Christianity in AD 366 and became intensely interested in the study of scripture and theology. After dedicating himself to the service of the Church, he spent most of his life translating the Bible from Hebrew, Aramaic, and Greek into Latin. You hold an English version of the Bible in your hands today because St. Jerome translated the ancient texts into Latin, from which most translations of the Bible are now written.

During his life, while working on these translations and spending countless hours diving into the text, St. Jerome said this: "Ignorance of scripture is ignorance of Christ." It's a famous line, spoken by an even more famous Church Father, who translated arguably the most famous of books. But what did he mean? Simply: if you don't know the Bible, then you don't know Jesus. But if you do read scripture, diving into it, plumbing its depths, and letting it permeate your life, then you will come to know and love the one whom the entire book is about. As you walk side by side with the one who knows you, loves you, and calls you to know and love him, you have to cling to the words that teach us about the Word. The journey is long, but the text you carry with you is an endless resource and abundant blessing that will help you know and love and follow Jesus.

3.

RECEIVE HIS GRACE

Let's review where we've been thus far. Prayer is how we approach Jesus and then grow in intimate union with him. The Bible is a beautiful compilation of stories and narratives that introduce us to the story of our life in God (what we call salvation history) leading up to Jesus and showing us his life and the founding of the Church. It's when we pray and read scripture that we are able to further grasp who Jesus truly is, meet him one-on-one, and grow to love him as he loves us.

But that's kind of where I get hung up. Prayer is essentially talking with Jesus, and reading scripture is learning about and listening to him. Jesus is someone I am called to meet and so are you. Of course, he's not physically standing right there when I pray or read the Bible. He's not in the room, sitting beside me in the pew, or answering phones at the parish's front desk like other people I know might be. But think for a moment about what makes a person a person. It is a far deeper reality than someone's body, right? Think about times when we know that someone is *with* us yet not physically present. He or she does not stop being a person and does in fact remain very real to us. We pray so we can share our hearts with Jesus, and we strive to hear the still quiet or eager calling of his voice and pursue intimate relationship with him. Our hearts are deeply moved and lives completely changed by encountering Jesus in prayer and scripture. Even still, the question lingers: Where is Jesus?

Developing a rich prayer life and reading the Bible regularly are noble, beautiful, and necessary tasks. These tasks engage our minds, generate new ideas, give us further understanding, and stir our emotions. But we are tactile, sensory people who use our minds in a physical world. We are physical beings with bodies *and* souls, and we cannot help but bring physicality to our mental activities. We fold our hands and bow our heads when we pray. We sit, stand, and kneel in Catholic gym class (also known as Mass). Our Bibles are printed, held in hands, and read aloud so we can hear them. We highlight our favorite passages and scribble in the margins. In pursuit of deeper understanding of Jesus, we take the mental practice and employ physical elements. This is who we are. It's part of our very being to want to engage in a physical and tangible way. We have a body and exist in a material world, which God made out of pure, unabashed love. He purposefully made us physical and spiritual, so we strive to give meaning and depth to both. We lift our hands as we share our hearts. We write our thoughts as we contemplate his word. We paint images that come to our mind as we picture the scene. We hold that printed Bible, turning those thin pages.

Jesus meets us in the physical world we inhabit. Jesus enters into our tactile, material existence to know us, love us, abide with us, and give us the chance to get to know, love, and follow him. This is the mystery and gift of the Incarnation: that the Word became flesh and dwelt among us. When we strive to meet and get to know Jesus, we're not trying to meet an idea, a character from the ancient book we call the Bible, or a theological concept that explains who God is. No, we are pursuing a relationship with a person who, even today, can be met and known, not only on a spiritual level but also in physical ways in and through the sacraments of the Church.

Jesus came here to pursue us, meet us, and give us life unending. We respond to that pursuit and receive all he has to give us in the

Church's sacraments. These encounters with Christ Jesus involve the assent of our minds, of course, but they also engage our physical selves. In other words, participating in the sacraments involves the whole of who we are—body, mind, and spirit. In the sacraments, we meet Jesus in water, light, and sacred oil. The Eucharist is bread and wine made Body and Blood. In the sacraments, especially in the Eucharist and Reconciliation (going to Confession), we draw closer to Jesus than through prayer and scripture alone, and we come to know more fully who he is.

JESUS' GRANDMA

I began babysitting in the ninth grade. A few of my mom's clients had young kids and some families from my parish knew me from youth group stuff, so I quickly built up a large clientele. Any given weekend, I was watching two or three kids while moms and dads snuck out for much-needed date nights. Thanksgiving, Christmas, and Easter breaks usually resulted in weeklong nanny sessions, and my summers were usually booked solid with different families day after day. It was the best job ever: cash for playing with cute kids.

I grew particularly close to one family, a family of four who were down-to-earth and fun. Also (let's be honest), they paid well. Mr. and Mrs. Jones were kind and hardworking, deeply faithful, and they had two of the most precious kids ever. Hunter was all boy: loved to be outside, loved his dog, and constantly talked about hunting and fishing. His little sister, Sophie, was the cutest thing on the block: curly blonde hair, deep-set blue eyes, and a belly laugh that could get the rest of the room giggling. I always jumped at the chance to watch them because it didn't feel like work; it was just fun that I happened to get paid to enjoy.

As Hunter and Sophie grew up, though, it became very evident to both kids that they could always get their way with me. I was hard-pressed to enforce nap time, I almost always caved when it came to giving them an extra snack. They knew I liked *High School Musical* just as much as they did, so I had no problem letting them watch it on repeat all afternoon. Knowing her kids were getting the best of me, Mrs. Jones made a deal with me for the longer days I watched them: if the kids were napping when she got home from work, I would earn an extra twenty bucks. That's no small amount of money at seventeen years old, so I did whatever I had to do to wear those kids out. But board game after board game, trips to McDonald's, and visits to the neighborhood pool were no match for their endless energy and seemingly infinite number of ways to convince me they didn't need a nap.

One particular afternoon, as I tried to negotiate with three-year-old Sophie to at least go shut her eyes for ten minutes (convinced she'd fall fast asleep and be napping for the last hour before her mom returned), she got a mischievous twinkle in her eye.

"Miss Katie, Miss Katie . . . I can't take a nap! Not yet! I gotta show you something!"

"Sophie, I've been to your house a lot. There's nothing here I haven't seen. You need to go take your nap."

"Nuh-huh!" She firmly pronounced, hands on her hips, head shaking. She spun around and ran off to her playroom. I reluctantly followed, figuring that if I went along with the nap-avoiding scheme for just a few minutes then I could maybe convince her to lie down after she'd shown me this new and exciting thing.

"Sophie, Hunter is in his room for quiet time. Don't you want to be like him? All grown up?"

"Nope! I want to play!" she shouted back. "Hurry! Up! I gotta show you something!"

I walked into the playroom, which we strangely enough hadn't used all day, and sure enough, it had been completely rearranged since the last time I'd gone in there just a few days before. Kid-friendly primary-colored shelves were installed along one of the walls, bins on each shelf holding a different type of toy. Two new bookshelves were covered with the ever-popular Berenstain Bears, Junie B. Jones, and Dr. Seuss books. A small flat-screen TV had been set up in the corner with kid-sized beanbags facing it. The room was a child's dream, a perfectly organized, well-stocked, little-kid heaven. But Sophie could not care less about all the playroom luxuries at that moment. Instead, she stood in the corner, proudly looking up at a framed sheet of paper covered with multicolored scribbles. The walls of the room were covered with Hunter and Sophie's art, a smattering of stick figures in a wide range of colors, all hung on the walls as if this was the Metropolitan Museum of Art of Lake Charles, Louisiana. But for some reason, Sophie was fixated on this one particular drawing.

It looked like she'd taken the caps off a pack of Crayola ten-count markers, stuck each marker on the paper at the exact same time, and just moved her hand back and forth in a circular motion. The paper was exploding with color. Running diagonally across the middle of the page was a black line. It was as if Sophie had taken the thickest permanent marker she could find and dug it into the paper with full force. You could see the indentation of the marker in the sheet. There was no rhyme or reason to the flow of the scribbles and no explanation for this thick black line. But still she stood there, beaming with pride as she looked up at what was clearly the picture she loved the most.

Hesitantly, I asked, "So . . . Sophie. What is it?" I tried to sound excited and curious all at once, but her little three-year-old-self saw right through me.

"Duh . . ." she said. "It's Jesus and his friends!" She proceeded to name the multicolored scribbly lines: there was Gus, Larry, and Joe. Can't forget Simba, Timone, and Pumba. And there was Buzz, Woody, and Nemo. Oh, good. We'd found him. I quickly realized that Jesus' friends all came from the Disney movie canon. Sophie was talking ninety miles an hour, proclaiming the backstories and relationships of each of these scribbly lines. Jesus was just a tiny red dot in the upper right-hand corner of the page. In Sophie's mind, Jesus just sat at the edge of the playground while his friends from Orlando played all around him.

As Sophie zoomed through her explanation of this complex portrait of Jesus' social life, she never identified the black line as anyone specific. The wheels in my head started spinning. Who could that be? Maybe one of the apostles? Or perhaps a Pharisee? And then it hit me: maybe the black line was Judas. Every hero needs a villain, right . . .

even a three-year-old knows that? Maybe Judas was cutting through Jesus and his friends, causing division and strife, which is why Jesus was hiding in the corner. I stood there, Sophie's voice drowning out as I deeply read into the meaning of this little girl's scribbly picture. Finally, after a solid two minutes of nonstop naming of each figure, Sophie took a deep breath.

"Hey, hang on, hang on!" I blurted out. "Sophie, who's the black line?" I asked. I just had to see if I was right about it being Judas.

She stared me down for nearly ten seconds before her eyes nearly went to the back of her head they rolled up so high.

"Uhhh, Miss Katie . . . that's Jesus' grandma," Sophie sighed, disappointment dripping from her little voice.

Before I even had the chance to laugh or ask further questions, she lost interest in her detailed explanation of this fine piece of three-year-old art and declared that she was tired and wanted to go take a nap. I breathed a sigh of relief at the thought of twenty extra bucks and a few moments to sit coming my way. After tucking her into bed, I found myself back in the playroom, staring up at the scribbly drawing.

I was confused. I totally understood why a three-year-old would draw a picture of Jesus and his friends. In her mind, the twelve apostles were just Jesus' friends, and every time she heard about Jesus, the apostles were involved. So clearly, in her mind, Jesus' friends were important and deserved to be drawn. But Jesus' grandma? What little kid has the presence of mind to contemplate the identity of Jesus' grandmother? How did she think to draw this woman in the first place? And better yet, why would she depict her as a black line cutting across all of Jesus' friends gathered together on a playground?

I stood there for a good half hour just staring at the picture, trying to process the fact that a young child I'd known since she'd been born had drawn a scene from Jesus' life that, while not necessarily depicted in scripture, could've been very real. It's been well over a decade since I saw that picture, but I've never forgotten it or the conversation I had with Sophie, because it revealed something remarkably profound: Jesus had a grandmother because he came here, to this physical, material world and lived a life just like us. He came here to invite us into deep, intimate communion with him. He came here, taking on human flesh and living a human life, precisely so that we could grow to know and love him and find salvation in him. He came here, and it took the wisdom of a three-year-old, some random scribbles, and a thick black line on an eight-by-ten sheet of printer paper to help me realize that.

HE LIVED AMONG US

As weird as it is to say or even think about, Jesus did have grandparents. Mary's parents, Joachim and Anne, are saints we honor and call upon to pray for us today. Jesus had friends, some we know the names of and some we don't. He had conversations with random strangers, ate dinner with the worst of sinners, and preached to influential men and women. Jesus spent time in people's homes, went to the Temple to pray, argued with Pharisees, and even strayed from his parents as a child. Jesus felt things deeply, weeping for his dead friend Lazarus and crying out in pain as he hung upon the Cross. I'm sure he smiled when he held small children on his lap, telling them stories and making them laugh. He was sad and angry, lonely and afraid. He was confident and hopeful, unafraid to say what needed to be said. Jesus is not a mythical figure relegated to stained glass windows in beautiful old cathedrals. He is not just some footnote in a textbook. Jesus—Son of God and Son of Man—became human, stepped into time, and is as real as we are, perhaps even more real than us, because he is God, our beginning and our end.

That should shock us. That should maybe even confuse us. I want to know why. Why did God become human in Jesus? Why would he enter into this mess we know as human existence? Why step into a world where people yell up at the sky in anger at you when a hurricane hits? Why dwell in a place where many deny your very existence? Why become flesh in a place where you will be brutally killed? Why would God bother with us in the first place?

Those questions have kept me up at night, although there's really a very simple answer: Jesus came here so we could know him, draw near to him, and so be saved. He stooped down to us so that we could be raised up to him. He came to meet us, and we must now take on the project of meeting him. How convenient, right? He came here to show himself to us so that we can truly grasp all that he is and all that he does. And somehow we forget this profound and beautiful truth as we go about our daily lives. Instead of reveling and living in that reality, we sometimes cram Jesus into the spare spaces of our hearts and minds and forget how deeply he loves us and how we are called to respond to his love. It is really very tempting to think of Jesus as a figure from history. We don't allow him to occupy the central and primary position he should, because we relegate him to the past. We sometimes just keep Jesus in our heads with our prayer or confine him to the pages of our Bible. We forget that while, yes, Jesus lived as a man in the ancient Middle East, he is also still here now. And we meet him in prayer, in scripture, and in the sacraments.

OUTWARD SIGNS; INWARD REALITY

The seven sacraments aren't just weird little rituals that we like to enact from time to time because we want to get dressed up or eat cake. They're not simple gestures to make us feel good, talk about God, or give us a chance to party. Sacraments are powerful and profound experiences of the very real, very necessary grace of God. When we are filled with that grace by participating in the sacraments, we are able to not only do all that is needed to meet Jesus daily and truly understand who he is, but we are also able to be in intimate, perfect communion with him. We become united to him through the physical things of our world such as water poured over one's head or into that one is immersed in Baptism, and the sacred chrism traced or poured on one's forehead in Confirmation, and the bread and wine that become the Body and Blood of Christ in the Eucharist. The infinite love and mercy of God and the person of Jesus come to us in these physical realities that we touch, smell, hear, see, and taste.

In the sacraments, Jesus Christ is someone we physically encounter. Thus the sacraments must be a priority for us, holding a unique place in our meeting and coming to know, love, and follow Jesus. When we participate in the sacraments, life-giving grace is poured forth. When we stand ready to receive that grace, we are transformed because we have encountered Jesus himself. We are receiving his very Body and Blood when we receive the Eucharist—we are consuming our Lord and Savior. When we go to Confession and receive the sacrament of Reconciliation, we are cleansed by the abundant mercy of Christ, who is present there in the person of the priest and the words of absolution. We are speaking to, and being spoken to by, Jesus. These two sacraments especially help us realize that Jesus isn't just that textbook figure, stained glass image, or character from the Bible. He is instead the one who gives, without fail, unending mercy, forgiveness, healing, and life-giving, soul-changing food. It's in the experience of the sacraments that our encounter with Jesus is something tangible, engaging all our senses, helping us to know him even more fully than we could have imagined or thought.

Far too often our attitude is that sacraments are just rituals. And while yes, there is a traditional ritual to the experience of the sacraments, they aren't merely obligations we are expected to keep. Rituals play an enormously important role in human life. Just think for a moment of your family rituals that surround holidays, birthdays, or other special occasions. Consider that rituals help facilitate real change in human life. Think about how the rituals surrounding a birthday help a family remember what has been, show gratitude for what is, and look forward in hope to what the coming year holds for the one whose birthday we celebrate and all those touched by his or her being alive. Rituals help us recall and learn more deeply who we are. The ritual celebrations of the sacraments do that in the most profound manner because they remind us of who we are as children of the Father and disciples of Christ Jesus. Sacraments bring real change by the graces we receive in and through them. The sacraments lead us deep into the very heart of Jesus, and we are fundamentally changed each time we receive them, becoming more and more the people God has created us to be. Each sacrament builds upon the others, for they work in union to fuel us further as we dive into the life-changing relationship with Jesus that we seek. They are not "one and done" activities, isolated on specific days. The sacraments are literally life-altering experiences that radically change us and help us meet Jesus in the very specificities and physicality of our lives.

When I ponder this reality of the physical nature of the sacraments, I think back to chemistry class in high school. Two of the three classes each week were lecture days. The teacher would stand at the front of the class and click through a fairly boring PowerPoint presentation, giving notes as we wrote down bullet point after bullet point. But day three was always lab day, when we got to wear old, yellowed lab coats and ugly safety goggles and blow things up. That's when those cursed and endless bullet points we'd all mindlessly written finally came in handy. Now we needed to know the concepts in order to actually do the experiments. We needed both: note days and experiment days. One without the other would've been an utter failure. Being able to see, in a visible way, and do, in a tangible way, experiments that showed us how certain chemicals reacted when we changed them in some way made equations far easier to solve and concepts more straightforward to grasp. The tactile experience was essential, even necessary, for every student in the class.

Our faith isn't so very different. We cry out for that which will put us ever closer to the God we cannot see with our physical eyes but want to meet and know intimately. We want a God who is physically present to us. We need our senses engaged, something tactile to help affirm what we grapple with in our mind about God and to reassure us of what we believe. The Seven Sacraments, each a beautiful and unique experience of God's divine life, are physical, tactile experiences that unite us to Christ Jesus.

FIRST CHANCE WE GET

In the fall of 2007, I returned home from college for the Thanksgiving break. I had only a couple days in town, so I set about scheduling every moment of my waking hours to ensure I saw the most people and enjoyed myself as much as I could. Wednesday evening, I went with a group of friends to a local restaurant for a little reunion. We hadn't seen each other since we'd all dispersed after graduation, so there was much to catch up on. I didn't get home until close to one o'clock in the morning. I knew we were leaving at nine o'clock to drive to my grandparent's house for the Thanksgiving meal, so I set my alarm for 8:00 a.m., collapsed on my bed, and drifted into dreamland. Just a few short hours later, I heard the television blaring from the kitchen, my dad whistling as he walked through the house, and my mom's voice bellowing through the halls, "Garland, have you seen my missal?"

In my half-asleep state, the thought crossed my mind, "Why does Mom have a weapon? And why did she lose it?"

I tried to stay asleep for as long as possible, but after the noise from downstairs grew louder as my sister joined my parents in the kitchen, I rolled over and out of bed. The clock read five o'clock, three hours earlier than my planned wake-up! I stormed down the stairs, furious that they were all awake and being loud.

"Why on earth are y'all up?" I shouted, as I huffed and puffed into the kitchen. "It is wayyyyy too early . . . and it's Thanksgiving!"

"Not my fault you stayed out late." Mom said, sipping her coffee as she read the newspaper.

"But it's your fault you're being so loud!" I snapped back. "Why are y'all up this early? It's a holiday!"

"Katie, don't speak to your mother that way," Dad said with a sigh, never lifting his eyes from the sports section.

For some reason, I was the only one outraged by this early morning breakfast. Taking a deep breath, I tried again.

"Why is everyone up so early? Did I miss something? Are we leaving early?" I asked, more calmly.

"We're going to morning Mass," Mom said, matter of factly.

"Isn't that at six thirty?" I asked. "Why are y'all awake an hour and a half before?"

"Because of the fast before Communion, Katie, duh" my sister said with a gigantic eye roll.

"You're welcome to come with us," Mom said again. "You're already up, aren't you?"

I stood there for a moment, looking at all three of them staring at each other. "This was a trick, wasn't it?" I shouted. "Y'all were loud on purpose! Just to wake me up!"

Mom, Dad, and Laura all started laughing. It had been one big plot: their banging around in the kitchen, their disinterestedness in my anger, their subtle and slow responses to my questions. All of it was meant to wake me up so I'd go to early Mass with them. I wanted to be mad but couldn't bring myself to blow up at them again. After all, I was home for just a couple days and I'd missed them.

"Fine," I said in utter defeat. "I'll go get dressed. Dad, can you fix me some peanut butter toast?" I asked, as I slowly walked out of the room, rubbing my tired eyes, longing for the three hours of sleep that had been stolen from me.

"Already in the toaster, sweetie." Dad called back, all three of them erupting in laughter again.

We went to Mass that morning as a family at six thirty, bright and early, four of only twenty-five people in the whole church. By 6:55 a.m. we were out the door and on the road to Grandma's house, where I finally ventured the question that had been on my mind since I'd realized they'd tricked me into waking up and going with them to Mass.

"Did y'all just want to leave earlier for Grandma and Papa's house, so y'all used waking up for Mass as the excuse?" It made sense. They didn't want me to be mad about leaving so early, so they used Mass as the ploy.

My mom twisted around from the front seat and stared me down. She wasn't mad, but she certainly wasn't happy I was accusing her of using Mass as a trick to get me out of bed.

"No, Katie. We wanted to go to Mass as a family, like we've been doing every morning at six thirty since September. And you're in town, so we definitely wanted to go with you. Why would today be any different?"

"Why'd y'all start going every morning?" I asked, puzzled and a bit confused as to where this new ritual had come from. We were Catholic, no doubt. Mass was important to us, as were all the other sacraments. We were there every Sunday, we were involved in parish ministries, and my parents tithed faithfully. But we'd never been the family that didn't ever miss, even on holidays designed to celebrate gratitude, football, food, and, in my mind, sleeping in. I just didn't know where this newfound, strict, morning-Mass-attending piety had come from.

There was a long pause as each of them tried to figure out a way to answer my question. My little sister, a high school freshman, had become wise beyond her years and remarkably clever for only fourteen years old. She finally said, "We go to morning Mass because Jesus is there. Why wouldn't we go to receive him the first chance we get?"

SOURCE AND MERCY

Jesus is there. He is there in that church. He is present in that building. He is physical and approachable in a small, seemingly insignificant piece of bread. And he wants us to be there too and to receive him in the Eucharist, which the Church tells us is the ultimate source and summit of our faith. He becomes part of us and we become part of him.

In the great mystery, gift, and sacrament of the Eucharist, Jesus transforms us from within to be like him. This is not just a nice symbolic gesture that just helps us feel connected to the Last Supper. It is Christ, made present to us through the Church's liturgy so that we can continue to participate in the perfect sacrifice he made with his death on the Cross.

Why wouldn't we rush to church then, every chance we get, to experience and receive him? Why wouldn't I wake up early on

Thanksgiving morning, or any morning for that matter, to run to the place where I know he is waiting for me so that I can come to know him even more fully and he can change me, bringing me closer to perfection in him? It's there, in the Church with the Eucharist, where we can have that physical experience of Jesus, an experience that we long for and that is essential to us.

We're transformed by this reception of the Eucharist, but even so, there are times when we stumble and fall, failing to live as if we've been changed by the encounter with Jesus. In those times of failure, we aren't supposed to go hide in shame, wallowing in our self-doubt and pain. We're called to approach Jesus with head bowed and heart sorrowful, ready to admit our mistakes and failures and ask for his forgiveness. We go to the sacrament of Reconciliation, humbly receiving the abundant mercy and unfailing love of Jesus Christ, who doesn't abandon us even when we willingly abandon him.

We're pursuing Jesus. We're on this adventure to meet him, walk with him, and know who he is, and then be changed by that knowledge. When we fail to keep our eyes fixed on him, we strike out on a different path, trying to create a different adventure for ourselves that's entirely contrary to what he has planned for us. At times we think we know what's best for ourselves, preferring our own ideas and living according to our own, self-focused agenda. That's all sin really is: choosing your own will over God's commandments. It's separating oneself from union with God and the work of his kingdom here on earth. Sin is when you make the temporarily pleasing choice rather than seeking God's eternal good. We aren't just left out in the cold when we do that, though. When we fail, Jesus doesn't just abandon us. There will certainly be moments when we approach Jesus ready to receive all he has to give, and there will be times when we mistakenly run in the opposite direction from him. Even when we've acted in ways that indicate we don't want to actually know him, Jesus is still there, ready to welcome us back into his loving arms.

His infinite goodness and perfect love is never hidden from or unavailable to us. We just have to approach him, ready to receive it. We have to place ourselves in his presence, humbly admit our sins, and ask to be forgiven. The sacrament of Reconciliation provides us the setting in which to do just this. We go to the confessional and sit before the priest, who is there for us as Christ's presence, and admit that we have done something that has pulled us away from God. We admit our sin, our sorrow, and our desire for healing. The priest absolves or frees us from our sin and we receive forgiveness.

These two very tangible, material experiences—the reception of the Body and Blood of Christ in the Eucharist and the experience of his abundant and merciful forgiveness in Reconciliation—should be priorities for you as you seek to truly know and love Jesus. We meet Jesus in the sacraments. We come to know him as we are transformed, from within, by our encounter with the physical elements of the Church's sacramental rituals, which Jesus instituted long ago. Mass every Sunday and Reconciliation once a year is required of all Catholics, but why limit yourself to that? If receiving the Eucharist and going to Confession aids you in meeting Jesus face-to-face, why not go as often as you can? You need Jesus. You want to get to know him. Here's how: you pray actively, you enter into the mystery of his life by reading the Bible, and you humbly approach the altar and the place of abundant, forgiving grace.

GOING TO GRACE

If Reconciliation and Eucharist are so critically important on this adventure with Jesus, then we must have a ready heart, open mind, and unflinching desire to experience the fullness of these gifts. We can't just be casual with the sacraments. Going to Confession cleanses our soul from sin. We're forgiven for the wrongs we've committed and brought back into right relationship with Jesus and his Church. To celebrate with our community at Mass and receive Christ, in the precious gift of the Eucharist, is the greatest honor and joy of our lives. We have to recognize the significance and beauty of the Eucharist and not just treat it as some simple ritual or rote obligation.

When we grasp the importance and necessity of these sacraments, we're compelled to spend time preparing to receive them and approach them worthily. The steps we take to prepare for and worthily experience these great gifts are critically important. Prepared hearts and ready minds become our perfect aids on this exciting adventure with Jesus.

RECONCILIATION: THE CHURCH'S HOSPITAL

How many times have you been to Reconciliation since your first time? When was the last time you received the sacrament of Reconciliation? How was the experience for you? Were you nervous, maybe unsure of what to say or how to start? Did you think the priest would judge you or make fun of your sins? Maybe you haven't been to Confession in a really long time. Why is that? Have you been scared? Do you know when it's offered at your parish? Or has it just kind of been in the back of your mind but not really a priority?

Wherever you fall on the "Confession spectrum"—scared to go, go once a year, go every week, or kind of forgot you were supposed to go in the first place—one thing is universal: we all need forgiveness and healing, and the sacrament of Reconciliation gives us that in abundance. One of the best ways to ensure that you're on top of going to Confession regularly, receiving those necessary graces, and basking in the mercy poured out upon you, is by taking time at the end of each day to think, process, and pray about what you've done (or haven't done) throughout that specific day. Think of this as a quick examination of conscience—maybe five or ten minutes—but long enough to help you contemplate where you've succeeded in your walk with Jesus and where you may have failed. If you find there are major issues and sins that have drawn you away from the Lord, you can put going to Confession on your calendar straight away.

Evening Examination of Conscience

- Find a quiet space (maybe your bedroom right before going to sleep) and eliminate distractions—turn off your phone and television, shut down your computer. Do whatever you have to do to focus only on your day and your walk with Jesus.
- Take a few deep breaths to settle yourself. If something is nagging at you and causing stress or anxiety, remind yourself that you can always think about that later or offer it up, give it to God in prayer. Try to clear your mind so that you can review your day little by little. Ask yourself questions such as these:
  → What was my attitude when I woke up this morning?
  → What were some of the first thoughts to cross my mind?
  → What was the first thing I said and did?
  → How did I treat the people I interacted with in the morning?
  → Did I pray this morning or acknowledge God's presence in my life?
  → Did I offer him my day? Ask him for help throughout it?

- Begin thinking about the things you did throughout the day: Did you go to work or school? Did you spend time at home? As you think about the specific activities that took place, go moment by moment and ask yourself:
  → Did I consider God's presence throughout my day?
  → Did I thank him for what was happening in my life or ignore him?
  → Did I strive to live virtuously and exhibit his love to other people?
  → Did I try to make life more joyful and easy for other people?
  → Was I prideful or arrogant at any point?
  → Did I tear others down or lift them up?
  → What was my attitude when things were asked of me?
  → Did I grumble and complain or was I willing to serve and work hard?

→ Did I think negative things about others or spread gossip today?

→ Was I jealous of other people and what they have? Or of their talents?

→ Was I respectful to those in authority (my parents, teachers, coaches, etc.)?

→ Did I trust the wisdom and guidance of others or stubbornly seek my own path?

→ Did I take time to pray today?

• As you're going through these questions, feel free to let your mind wander into specific moments and interactions. Replay conversations with different people. Contemplate how certain moments made you feel and what you thought. It's only when we truly reflect on what has happened that we can become more aware of what we have done. You may begin to realize consistent patterns of making mistakes, which means you'll be able to more easily course-correct in the future.

• After you've pondered these questions and thought about your day, pray the following:

> Lord, thank you for the day you have given me.
> Forgive me of the sins that have distanced me from you.
> I will work to do better tomorrow.
> I give you glory for all you have done for me.
> Amen.

If you go through this brief examination daily, you'll begin to develop the ability to become aware of your most frequent sins. You'll become reflective and can take note of where you stumble the most. If every day you find that you're answering yes to the question "Did I gossip?" then you can start thinking about who you're with when you gossip, what kind of topics lead you into gossip, and why it may be so easy for you to spread gossip. Then you can start to take steps to avoid these situations, people, or moments. You can begin to repent from the repetitive sin, which is what our goal should always be: to be free from that which is pulling us away from Jesus. When you notice these frequent sins, you can head down a path of heartfelt conversion.

The start of that journey begins in the Church's hospital: the confessional. We are sinners, which means we have turned away from God and have stopped being who he has created us to be. When we make decisions that separate us from the fullness of his love and mercy we create barriers between ourselves and God and that leads to a sort of illness in one's soul. If we're going to know Jesus intimately, then we have to admit what we've done that has made us sick—that has drawn us away from his love.

So ask yourself each day, "What have I done to barricade myself from God's abundant love? What have I done to avoid meeting Christ?" Remember, that's all sin is: decisions we have made, purposefully and selfishly, that have created distance from the presence of God. Sin is when we walk away from Jesus. Confession is when we walk right back in, say we're sorry, and strive to do better.

Monthly Confession

It's good to develop the habit of going to Confession at least monthly. If you find, through your evening examination, that there is a serious sin hounding you, then get to the sacrament of Reconciliation—even if it's right after having gone or it's earlier in the month than you would usually go. Receiving the sacrament regularly helps ensure that you become more comfortable with what can sometimes be scary or intimidating. To walk into a room, close the door, and list for a priest all the things you did wrong sounds neither fun nor exciting. In fact, it rather seems like an unpleasant, inconvenient activity.

But—and this is critically important to understand—the sacrament of Reconciliation is given to us by Jesus Christ, established in the scriptures as the means by which the things we have done wrongly on earth will be loosed and forgiven in heaven. When we go to Confession, we are approaching God himself and asking forgiveness so that we can return to an intimate relationship with him. That's all it is: an outpouring of God's grace upon us as we admit fault and ask forgiveness for the wrong we have done. God gives that grace and mercy freely, if only we approach, ask, and resolve to do better next time. So we walk into that confessional, confident that our sins are forgiven through the power of the priest, who acts as Christ when he receives our confessions, accepts our contrition, and grants us forgiveness. We walk into the confessional confident that God the Father has reconciled the world to himself through the death and Resurrection of Jesus.

If we want to get to know Jesus, we have to make sure the lives we lead are filled with moments that bring us to him, not draw us away. When we fail at this, we rush to the sacrament of Reconciliation to get us back on track.

A nightly examination of our conscience forms the good habit of reflection and self-awareness so that we can become conscious of our sins. When you take the time to go to Confession once a month, it's helpful to do a longer examination of conscience, one that takes you through each of the Ten Commandments and asks pointed, specific questions to help you truly examine the moments you succeeded in your walk with Jesus and the moments you strayed.

It can be helpful to enter into a deeper time of examining your conscience by reading one of the most popular parables Jesus ever used: the Parable of the Prodigal Son in Luke 15:11–32. The story is probably familiar to you: The younger of two sons goes to his wealthy father and asks for his half of the estate and then leaves to go spend the money on wild living. In other words—he takes a gift given to him and wastes it. That's what "prodigal" means, after all—wasteful. The young man eventually finds himself broke and alone, living among the pigs of a local farmer. This point shouldn't be overlooked: he's a Jewish man living among pigs, an animal considered unclean in Judaism. He has hit rock bottom. He's lost it all, has nowhere to turn, and nothing to his name. So he decides to try and go home, hoping that at the very least the father who gave him half the estate will let him work as a servant. The son doesn't expect much. He's not hoping to be brought back into the family or even greeted with any sort of joy or celebration. He just doesn't want to live with the pigs and is willing to work to prove that he made a mistake. But the father doesn't just cast his wasteful son aside and berate him for his stupidity and failures. When he sees him coming up the path, the father runs out to meet him on the road and showers him with affection and joy. The father throws a party to welcome his son home, and declares that his son was once dead but is now brought back to life. The father forgives the wasteful son who took his inheritance and misused it without hesitation. He doesn't place conditions upon the forgiveness either. He just hugs his son, brings him back into the family, and showers him with love.

God does the same to us when we go to the sacrament of Reconciliation. He welcomes us back into his loving arms when we enter into the confessional and humbly and sorrowfully admit our faults and ask forgiveness, resolving to do better in the future. As you go through this examination of conscience, don't beat yourself up. Don't make yourself feel bad. Be intentional in your reflection, but be hopeful in your belief that when you honestly confess your sins, you will be met by the loving arms of Jesus Christ, who wants to welcome you home and continue this adventure.

Longer Examination of Conscience

- The First Commandment: I am the Lord your God: you shall not have strange gods before me.
  → Did I serve God willingly or slowly and grudgingly?
  → Did I neglect my prayer life? Did I avoid sharing my heart with God?
  → Have I made other things in my life (material, spiritual, personal, social) more of a priority than God? What have those things been? Why did they take priority over God?
  → Have I engaged in anti-Christian activities or participated in activities such as reading horoscopes, engaging in the occult, fortune-telling, palm reading, or astrology?
  → Did I publicly or privately say I don't believe in God?

→ Have I purposefully led myself or others away from God with what I've said, done, or shared?

- The Second Commandment: You shall not take the name of the Lord your God in vain.
    → Have I cursed? Why did I? What words did I say and in what context?
    → Did I take God's name in vain? Did I use God's name mockingly, jokingly, angrily, or without reverence? Did I do this with the Blessed Virgin Mary or any other saint?
    → Did I mock crucifixes, rosaries, icons, or holy objects or misuse them in any way? Did I break a promise I had made or purposefully lie?

- The Third Commandment: Remember to keep holy the Lord's Day.
    → Did I purposefully skip Mass on a Sunday or holy day of obligation?
    → Was I disrespectful to the celebration of Mass by not participating, showing up excessively late, dressing inappropriately, or mocking the service?
    → Did I allow myself to become excessively distracted in Mass, only going through the motions and not truly investing myself in the experience? Did I distract others?
    → Did I fail to fast one hour before receiving Communion?
    → Have I mocked or disrespected Mass?
    → Did I allow myself to become overly busy and overworked on Sunday and avoid spending time in rest, prayer, and with family and friends?

- The Fourth Commandment: Honor your father and mother.
    → Was I disobedient to my parents or others in authority over me?
    → Did I avoid helping my parents when they needed me? Did I avoid spending time with my parents and family?

→ Have I disrespected my family? Did I disregard their affection, care, guidance, and leadership? Have I had a bad attitude?

→ Did I participate in the activities of my family and help around the house?

• The Fifth Commandment: You shall not kill.

→ Did I easily lose my temper or get angry?

→ Did I attempt to injure or be purposefully violent toward other people? Was I reckless with driving or in other activities?

→ Did I lead others into sin by telling mean-spirited or inappropriate jokes, dressing in a provocative manner, or inviting someone to something immoral?

→ Did I gossip and damage the reputation of others? Did I cause scandal with things I said about other people? Did I use social media, texting, or technology to tear down others or spread rumors?

→ Did I contemplate suicide or try to physically harm myself in any way?

→ Have I consumed food or drink in excessive amounts?

→ Did I participate in physical violence? Did I consent to or advise someone in an abortion?

→ Have I caused harm to others with my words or actions?

→ Did I desire revenge or harbor hatred toward others?

→ Did I fight with others unnecessarily?

• The Sixth Commandment: You shall not commit adultery.

→ Did I entertain lustful or impure thoughts? Did I act upon those thoughts and violate purity and chastity in my life?

→ Did I have impure or inappropriate conversations?

→ Did I look at pornography or engage in masturbation? Did I actively engage in activities that compromised my purity? Did I view inappropriate things online? Did I share those things with others?

→ Did I dress or act immodestly? Did I act upon lustful and impure thoughts?

→ Have I placed myself in situations that compromise my purity and living chastely?

- The Seventh Commandment: You shall not steal.
  → Did I take things that are not mine? What were they? Why?
  → Did I knowingly and willfully damage other people's property?
  → Did I deceive someone when it came to money or property?
  → Have I borrowed something from a family member or friend with no intention of returning it?
  → Was I greedy? Lazy? Wasteful with time and resources?
  → Did I spend money I don't have? Have I accumulated debts that I can't pay back?

- The Eighth Commandment: You shall not bear false witness against your neighbor.
  → Did I tell lies on purpose? Did I damage others with my lies? Did I damage my own life by lying?
  → Have I unjustly accused other people?
  → Did I tell the faults and secrets of other people without necessity?
  → Did I tell derogatory lies about others or spread falsehoods and rumors through gossip?
  → Did I reveal a secret shared with me in confidence?

- The Ninth Commandment: You shall not covet your neighbor's wife.
  → Have I thought impure things about other people?
  → Did I wish that someone else would like or love me more than other people?
  → Did I act upon lust in my heart and mind?

- The Tenth Commandment: You shall not covet your neighbor's goods.
  → Have I been envious and jealous of what other people have, to the point of wishing they did not have it themselves?
  → Have I attempted to take what is not mine out of jealousy?

→ Did I tear others down because I wanted what they have?

→ Have I vandalized or ruined other people's property or things?

I find it helpful to keep a small notebook or piece of paper with me when I do a longer, in-depth examination of conscience so I can write down my sins. (Obviously I destroy that thing the second I leave the confessional!) Writing down my sins makes them concrete and makes me confront exactly what I have done that has led me away from Jesus, which then acts as a further encouragement to not do it anymore. I don't want to write down those things again. Instead, I want to make a greater effort to stay the course with him on this great adventure of meeting and knowing him day by day.

A Regular Confessor

If you start getting in the habit of going to Confession each month, it may be helpful to try to go to the same priest each time so you can build a relationship of trust and he can help you recognize patterns in your life. Just like a nightly examination of conscience can show you areas of consistent struggle, confessing to the same priest each month can give you advice that builds. Many parishes have their regular Confession times posted in the bulletin or parish website. Add that time to your calendar and try to consistently go with the same priest each time. This is, of course, an ideal, not a requirement, but you may find that it quickens your efforts to return to the path where you are meeting and coming to know Jesus.

THE EUCHARIST: OUR FUEL

The Eucharist is the source and summit of our Catholic faith. It is our beginning and our end, the heart of the Church. In the celebration of the Eucharist we join ourselves to the saving mystery of the Death and Resurrection of Jesus. Through the liturgical action of the Mass and the person of the priest, simple bread and wine become the Body and Blood of Christ, what we know as the Real

Presence. This profound mystery of our faith requires our reverence, humility, and receptivity to the fullness of grace.

So why then do we treat Mass like an optional activity sometimes? Or take Communion as the signal for a quick bathroom trip before Mass ends? Why do we sometimes approach the greatest gift given to us as some commonplace, weekly activity instead of the high point of our week and the very foundation of our entire adventure with Jesus?

The answer is simple: we don't always take the time to contemplate or appreciate all the Eucharist is, nor do we give adequate time to actively prepare our hearts to receive Jesus in this most precious gift. Christ Jesus comes to us at Mass. He is present in the person of the priest, in the Word proclaimed, in the activities of the assembled faithful, and most especially in the eucharistic species of bread and wine. Nothing is more important, nothing more valuable, and nothing more necessary if we want to meet him and get to know him. So what can we do to ensure that we take the Eucharist seriously, treating it as the high point and foundational experience that it is?

Eucharistic Adoration: A Chance to Sit with Jesus

When I was a kid, once a month my parents would call a babysitter to come watch my sister and me so they could go out on a date. We'd always whine and fuss when they left because we wanted to go with them, but my mom and dad were pretty stuck in their ways: this was their date night, for just the two of them. It wasn't until I got married that I realized just how critically important that date night probably was for them: they needed time together. Married for more than thirty years now, my parents still go on dates (though now more regularly since both kids are out of the house!). It's a priority for them, and for many couples, to take time to just be together—to talk, to listen, to reconnect. In the hustle and bustle of daily life, time spent together can be renewing and refreshing, and it's necessary for the relationship to thrive.

Think about your friends—you spend time with them, don't you? You do things together. You regularly talk and text. If you didn't do those things, the friendship would falter and fizzle out. This is why we pray . . . we talk to the Lord and we lift up our hearts. We communicate with him, and then we take the time to listen. One of the best places to do that—one of the best ways to spend time with Jesus one-on-one (just like the married couple that goes on regular dates)—is in eucharistic adoration.

There is a long tradition in the Church of adoring Christ present in the Eucharist outside of Mass. We reserve the Blessed Sacrament in a tabernacle for two reasons: first is so that it is available to take to those, particularly those near death, who cannot come to Mass because of illness or other reasons. The second reason is so that members of the faithful can pray before the Blessed Sacrament in eucharistic adoration. In this devotional practice, you sit before the tabernacle and meditate, pray, and perhaps read scripture. There is another form of eucharistic devotion known as Exposition, which is when the Blessed Sacrament is displayed in a monstrance. This is accompanied by a simple ritual of prayers and often hymns led by a priest. Some parishes offer adoration with the Rosary, or praise and worship music, or a Divine Mercy chaplet. Some parishes even offer perpetual adoration—a chapel that is open 24/7—and people sign up for an hour of prayer at a time and go regularly. There are even places that do adoration directly before and after Mass, giving people even more time to contemplate and enter into the mystery of the Eucharist.

Try to find time to go to adoration, maybe once a month. Just like the couple who makes time for their date night, away from home, work, and the busyness of daily life, you can take intentional time to just go and be with Jesus. When you take that time, bring your Bible. You might read through the book of Psalms or the gospels while you're there and incorporate lectio divina. The Rosary is a great tool to use to enter into a time of meditation and rest with Jesus, especially since it's so repetitive and familiar. Sometimes it's valuable to just sit and be with Jesus, not necessarily doing or saying anything other than enjoying being in his presence. Far too often, we make ourselves busy with Jesus, forgetting that the best way to truly meet and get to know him is to just simply be ourselves with him.

There's a famous story of St. John Vianney, a priest in France who was pastor of a small country parish. Every morning, he'd walk into the church and a peasant would be sitting in the front row, staring at the tabernacle where the Blessed Sacrament was reserved. And every day, John Vianney would wonder who this man was and why he was always sitting in the front row, staring at the tabernacle. So one day, John asked the man, "What are you doing when you sit here in this church day after day?" The peasant told St. John Vianney, "Well, I look at Jesus, and Jesus looks at me."

That's all adoration of the Blessed Sacrament is: you looking at Jesus, and Jesus looking at you. In something as small, simple, and vulnerable as a piece of bread is contained the body, blood, soul, and divinity of the one we want to meet and get to know. Spending time with him can only help us come to know him personally and grow close to him.

Preparing for Mass

When we go to Mass, we should not just treat it as a weekly required activity to keep our parents happy or to satisfy some cosmic to-do list that the heavenly powers keep on file. It should be the very highlight of our week when, together with our local community, we listen and learn from the scriptures, the homily, and our hymns. We offer praise and thanksgiving to the Father through the Son and intercede for the needs of the world. Sunday Mass is the center of our life as Catholics, the point at which we offer ourselves, including our sinfulness, to God and in return receive healing, food for our journey, and Christ himself when we partake of Holy Communion. Sunday Mass is both a time to end one week, offering it all to God, and to prepare for all that is to come in the following week. We have to see the Mass as the most valuable experience of our week, every single week.

For years, my parents have served as extraordinary ministers of Communion at our parish, and so when Mass was finished on Sundays, a lot of times they were in the sacristy helping Father clean up.

A small, framed sign hangs on the wall of the sacristy. I've seen it all my life, having gone back there to wait for my parents after Mass, yet it's only been in recent years that I've appreciated how profound the statement is. It reads, "Celebrate this Mass as if it's your first Mass, your last Mass, and your only Mass."

That should be our attitude every time we go to Mass and receive Jesus in the Eucharist—as a singularly important, valuable, precious moment. And we need to prepare for that valuable moment. No different than when we get dressed up for a date, clean the house if guests are coming over, or study for a big exam, we prepare for those things that are important. Mass is the most important event, the Eucharist the most precious gift, we have because offering ourselves to Jesus and receiving him under the signs of bread and wine is the closest we will ever be to him . . . so we must prepare! Then, once we have prepared, we must enter fully into the experience. We don't just go to Mass to go through the motions. We must lift our voices in song—even if we sing off-key. We must respond with vigor and passion—even if everyone around us is just mumbling. We must approach the liturgy with great respect and reverence, recognizing what an awesome gift we've been given by being able to pray, sing, and worship our Lord in the Mass.

Read the Readings Early

The Mass consists of two main parts: the Liturgy of the Word and the Liturgy of the Eucharist. The first "half" of the Mass is when we hear the Word of God proclaimed and listen to the guidance and wisdom of the priest or deacon in the homily. How often do we zone out, though? The homily may get too long, or the readings may have far too many funny names in them and don't seem at all relatable. By reading the assigned Mass readings of the day ahead of time, it's easier to really engage with what's happening in this first part of the Mass. There are a number of apps you can download on your phone that'll give you access to the assigned readings (just Google "Catholic Mass readings" and a ton of options will come up). Or you can simply visit www.usccb.org and use the calendar on the side of the screen to bring you straight to that day's readings. Or grab a missal on the way into Mass and read them before Mass begins, just so you've seen them at least once before you hear them proclaimed.

On a Sunday, there is a first reading (usually from the Old Testament); a psalm, which is meant to be sung, but at times is read; a second reading (usually from a letter of St. Paul); and the gospel reading. These four pieces of biblical texts won't take you very long to read, but you should definitely take time to contemplate and pray with each passage. Use the lectio divina method outlined in chapter 2, or work your way through these questions below to help you dive deeper into each passage:

- What connection do I see between the readings? Is there a theme or concept that seems to be common between each one?
- What am I feeling as I read these readings? What seems to be stirring in my heart and mind? Can I relate to any of the individuals in the stories? Are certain situations familiar to me?
- Am I encouraged by these words? Am I having a hard time appreciating or focusing on what these passages are saying? If so, why?
- What would I say in a brief homily about these readings? What message would I share with others about what is happening in each passage?

Remember, you're stepping into the Mass with an understanding of the readings about to be proclaimed, which can help you stay focused and perhaps even aid you in noticing new things as you hear them again. When you are prepared for and tuned into the Liturgy of the Word, your mind is elevated and your heart is stirred with a gratitude for the beauty of this part of the Mass. The Word is first being proclaimed so that you can further understand and even appreciate what is about to be given to you in the Eucharist. Further, this first experience of the Word of God can stir within us a desire to give of ourselves as the Lord is about to be given to us.

Homily Notes

A little boy was giving the priest a high five after Mass, and the priest said, "Well, young man, what was your favorite part of Mass today?" Without missing a beat, the little boy said, "When you stopped talking and sat down."

How often is that our own attitude? We give Father So-and-So five minutes to talk, and if he doesn't wow us, make us laugh, bring us to tears, or shock us with his wisdom, then we tune out and start staring at the clock. In all fairness, not every priest is the best homilist in the world. They can't all be eloquent preachers with simultaneous stand-up comedy and theology professor backgrounds. But they are holy men who have been called by God and the Church to guide their flocks, and the words they share with us on Sunday are important. We should find ways to pay attention to them.

The same way reading the readings ahead of time can help us focus and tune in to how Jesus wants to speak to us, when we are intentional in our listening to the homily, we can more intensely hear the voice of the Lord. One of the best ways to do this is by getting a small notebook and taking a few short notes during the homily so you can go back and think about them later on. Now, don't misunderstand: this is not buying a five-subject college-ruled notebook and filling it up with perfect dictation of what Father says (although you could if you'd like). No, this is just simply taking note of a few things that really stick out to you. The same way you thought about the readings when you read them early and maybe noticed themes that struck you and began contemplating the deeper meaning behind each passage, so too will the homily point things out that may tug at your heart and help you grow closer to Jesus. But how often do we walk out after Mass with those simple points totally forgotten? If we jot these things down, then later that same day we can go back to the readings and perhaps read them again, look at what the priest said, and enter into a time of personal, spontaneous prayer focused on asking Jesus to help us live out the message or lessons learned during the coming week. Remember Sunday is both ending and beginning.

Ask Jesus to help you make the Liturgy of the Word a lasting and life-changing part of your coming week.

Halftime Offering

After the homily, we have what I've affectionately nicknamed "holy halftime." During the offertory of Mass, we hit the halfway point of the celebration. The Liturgy of the Word is finished and the altar is being prepared for the Liturgy of the Eucharist. Ushers are passing baskets, moms are taking fussy kids to the bathroom, the choir is singing a song. There's a lot of movement and activity at this point, and it's easy to become distracted, lose focus, or just think you can begin to zone out.

But this is not just a transition time of the Mass. This isn't the chance to just get up and stretch your legs, check your phone, or let your mind wander to whatever you want to have for brunch when you get home simply because nothing is being said at the front. This is the perfect time to go back through those readings, ponder the homily, and ask yourself what you want to offer to Jesus during this time. Beginning with the offertory and continuing throughout the Eucharistic Prayer, we offer ourselves—and what's happening in our lives—to the Lord. This is why people from the congregation bring up the gifts: the people in worship—in Mass—are bringing what is needed to Jesus, and it will be transformed into something profoundly beautiful and necessary for us.

So we need to bring up our own gifts. While not necessarily in a physical sense, as in walking up to the altar, we need to bring to the Father through Jesus what's going on in our lives and that which we'd like him to transform. As the bread and wine will become the Body and Blood of Christ, we too will become once again—will be reconstituted as—the Body of Christ. By the eucharistic sacrifice, we will be returned to our truest selves as Christ's hands and feet, present and acting in our world.

If you need help focusing during the collection, the offertory procession, and/or the preparation of the gifts and altar, then pray through the following questions. Better yet, make these part of your preparation for Mass before you get to church or when you first arrive, before the opening hymn.

- What's going on in my life right now? With my family? With my friends? At school? At work?
- What can I give to Jesus to bring to the Father to be healed, transformed, or made whole?
- What gift or talent can I offer up to Jesus this week and use for the sake of his kingdom?
- Who in my life needs prayers right now? How can I bring them to Jesus right now?

Be intentional during the offertory. Really use it as a chance to offer yourself—all that you are and all that you could be—so that you can more fully enter into the most beautiful and important thing we can ever hope to experience: the Eucharist.

The Eucharistic Prayer

There isn't enough ink in the world that could be spilled to explain how profoundly beautiful and necessary the Eucharistic Prayers are. We've heard these words hundreds of times, so often in fact that we kind of go through the motions and mumble the responses. What if, instead, we treated each Mass like that little sacristy sign said we should: as if it's the first, the last, and the only? Wouldn't we hang on every word the priest says? Wouldn't we very prayerfully utter our responses, knowing that the words we say are meant to be heartfelt, meaningful prayers exposing our need and desire to receive Jesus fully in what is about to be transformed for and given to us?

During the Eucharistic Prayer, which is the heart of the second part of the Mass, be purposeful in listening to every word the priest prays. Offer your responses with passion and loudly enough to be heard. Don't just mutter or mumble along with the crowd. These are your words spoken back to the one who is both speaking to us and about to be consumed by us. When we say we are lifting our hearts to the Lord, are we really doing that? Are we giving thanks for all he has given us because it is right and just to do so? Are we singing the words "Holy, Holy, Holy" with the choirs of angels, or are we glancing at our watch yet again because we know there's not much longer to go? Invest yourself fully in the words prayed because this is when simple bread and wine become Christ. And even with all our brokenness we are invited to come forward and receive him who is made present for us.

You also might talk with your pastor, another staff member at your parish, or someone else who has studied the Church's liturgy about how to learn more about the Eucharistic Prayers. They have roots in the very first decades of Christianity. They have fascinating histories, and convey amazing truths of our faith. Listening to these prayers of thanksgiving and offering will start to mean more to you as you pay closer attention and learn more about them.

Receiving the Eucharist

As people begin to line up to receive Communion, we tend to let our eyes wander around the room. I usually find myself staring at people's shoes as they walk back to their pews, and I completely forget that I'm supposed to be preparing myself to walk up to receive Jesus himself. We will never be closer to Jesus in this earthly life than when we literally place him in our mouth and consume the Eucharist. It is a direct answer to the question "How can I meet Jesus?" You can receive the Eucharist. You can bring him into yourself. And then you have met him. You have allowed him to become part of you. You have approached him, you have consumed him, and he is now going to transform you. A great prayer to use to help you contemplate this mystery is the Preparation for Mass prayer written by St. Thomas Aquinas (which can easily be found online). I've gotten into the habit of praying this simple prayer as I kneel and wait to enter the Communion line. It's very repetitive and straightforward, covering all the bases of what I hope receiving this Eucharist will do in my life both in that moment and in the ones to come.

Nothing is more beautiful (or simple) than that moment: to walk up to another human person and receive Christ into our very bodies.

We have to ensure our hearts and minds are ready for this. We heard the Word of God proclaimed. We paid attention to what the priest had to say. We offered up our hearts during the time of preparation. Now, all of that combined allows us to step into line, welcome Christ, and accept the mission that life in him requires of us, namely to go out and change our world by being his presence in it.

- As you kneel, waiting to go and receive the Eucharist, begin thinking about the readings again—especially the common theme.
- Ask yourself how that theme and the words spoken by the priest can challenge you in the coming week. Ask Jesus to let this reception of his Body and Blood be the fuel and strength you need to live out the truth proclaimed and to give you fortitude to continue walking in faith.
- When you get in line to receive Communion, begin reciting these simple words attributed to St. Augustine: "Lord, you are the Bread of life. You give your very self to me. In this eucharistic bread, I receive what I am—the Body of Christ—so that I may become what I receive—the Body of Christ."
- After you've received Communion and you find yourself in the pew once again, there is no better time than this to pour your heart out to Jesus. He dwells within you. Now, more than ever, you can open yourself entirely to him, asking for his aid, protection, guidance, support, and strength. Now is the perfect time to express your joys and desires, to thank him for the good works he has already done in your life, and to petition him for help along your journey. Jesus has allowed himself to become so small that he is within you. So you are able to now offer yourself even more to him by lifting your mind and heart during this time and allowing Christ within you to transform you.

GO FORTH

We don't experience the Mass (or any sacrament) in a vacuum. It's not a compartmentalized experience where we do one thing, then the next, then the next. The readings at Mass speak to our hearts as we hear the Word of God. Those readings inform and guide the homily, and what touches us in the homily should stir our hearts in prayer during the offertory. What we lift up to the Lord is sanctified and blessed upon the altar of Jesus' sacrifice, and we are able to fully enter into the mystery of his Incarnation, Death, and Resurrection. Each moment of the Mass—precious, unique, and beautiful—draws us close to Jesus. The readings tell us his story, the homily unpacks ways we can encounter him, and Communion gives us the awesome chance to receive him into ourselves and be as close to him then as we ever will be in our earthly life. This is all meant to transform us completely so that, in a very real way, we can become the hands and feet of Jesus. We become his body in the world as we receive his body into our own.

Similarly, we don't go to Reconciliation just to check the sins off our dirty laundry list and then return to our regularly scheduled program of sinning, confessing, and then sinning again. We're transformed by the experience—washed clean, filled with the abundant grace of forgiveness, and meant to live differently as a result of that encounter with the merciful God. The experience within that hospital of mercy changes us from the inside out. We leave that room having met Jesus, who emboldens us to be different—perhaps even sharing what we have experienced because we now know Jesus for ourselves.

When the priest or deacon says the words, "Go forth, the Mass has ended," or "Go forth, proclaiming the Gospel with your lives," or whatever variation of the closing words are that day, we proudly and prayerfully say, "Thanks be to God." When the priest says, "I absolve you of your sins," we confidently say, "Amen." That doesn't mean we just get to go back to our normal routines, our regular lives, or our typical sins. We are affirming that we are, thankfully, able to go out and proclaim, share, witness to, and teach what has happened within the walls of that church. We have met Jesus, and now we can share that immeasurably powerful moment with others. We are declaring with confident belief that a great work of mercy has been done for us and that we are empowered to go and sin no more, showing the world that meeting Jesus and coming to know him leads to a different life, filled with virtue rather than sin.

We attend Mass, adore Christ in the Blessed Sacrament, and receive the sacrament of Reconciliation over and over again. We live the sacramental life precisely so that we can become sacraments ourselves—physical manifestations of the grace of God in the world. We go to church so we can go *be* the Church. We meet Jesus there so we can share him and help others meet him too.

4.

SHARE THE GIFT

We meet Jesus in prayer. We come to know him by reading the Word of God. We consume him and are transformed by him in the sacramental life of the Church. Those moments of our lives shouldn't be kept secret or even private. Your relationship with Jesus is given not for you alone but for the life-saving mission of the Church and the sake of the world. No, we're not necessarily called to climb up on a cafeteria table and yell to everyone in the room, "I'm praying now!" just so they know how much we love Jesus. But on the other hand, we shouldn't hide from others that we pray and that it is an essential part of our daily lives. I'm not demanding that you wave your Bible around in English class and shout, "Repent, the kingdom of God is at hand!" every time you read a parable or pray through a psalm. But the fact that you steep yourself in scripture and allow those words to be a lamp unto your feet shouldn't be a massive secret to those who know and love you. I don't think you need to add your entire Confession to your Snapchat story (that would just be weird), but people should know that you value the great gift of that sacrament and go to it frequently because you know you need God's mercy if you want to be in relationship with him.

If you've come to meet and know Jesus because you've talked to him in prayer, seen his life as you've read the Bible, and been fueled by the transforming grace bestowed upon you in the sacraments, then you can't keep that to yourself. Your encounter with Jesus is one that must be shared. The lifting of your heart, the listening to his Word, and the reception of perfect sacramental gifts compel you to share Jesus with others. You've been transformed by your encounter with him, and that gives you immeasurable strength to then serve him— and others—in the most perfect way possible: by witnessing to who Jesus is and helping others meet him too.

STOPPING TRAFFIC

As we made our descent into LAX around noon, we could see the traffic covering the 405. Arguably the most log-jammed interstate in America, I immediately knew we had a good two-hour car ride ahead of us once we landed, and I silently (and selfishly) prayed that maybe we'd pick up some food before getting entangled in all that mess. My friend Teresa picked us up at Terminal 4, her little Mazda SUV stuffed to the gills with boxes of T-shirts and name tags. Tommy and I crammed our luggage in the open nooks and crannies of the car and climbed in, ready to set out for the UCLA campus to speak at the Diocese of Los Angeles's City of Saints Youth Conference.

"We've just got one more person to grab," Teresa said, as she took off to Terminal 2. "His flight was delayed, so he just got here, which is perfect, because now we can all go to lunch together!"

I breathed a sigh of relief. Lunch was on the agenda, thank goodness. A few minutes later, a man wearing a gray friar's habit climbed into the front seat of the little SUV with a backpack, small suitcase, and guitar case. A simple brown rope with a giant rosary dangling down was wrapped around his waist. His gray-speckled beard matched his habit, the hood of which was flapping in the gush of wind as he slammed the door. He leaned over and gave Teresa a hug and kiss on the cheek before turning around and smiling at Tommy and me in the back seat.

"Hey!" he said loudly, a giant smile crossing his face. "I'm Fr. Agustino. Who are y'all?" His energy was unmatched and we instantly liked him.

After introducing ourselves, swapping basic information about where we lived and what we did, the conversation quickly shifted to what we could expect for the upcoming weekend. Teresa filled us in on simple details—the schedule, where we were staying, how many teens were registered for the conference. We heard about the history of the event and why they wanted to create it for the archdiocese. She told us how important it was for the archbishop to make sure the young people in Los Angeles were evangelized and how this was an event he had personally requested to create. He wanted the Gospel spread—he wanted this to become a city of saints, filled with young people who had met Jesus. At every new piece of information, Fr. Agustino nodded his head with great vigor, saying simply, "Cool. Cool!" and occasionally dropping in a "This is going to be so great!" I had never met someone who radiated such joy, even after having spent most of his morning sitting in an airport waiting for a delayed flight. He had this presence about him, as if nothing—even four hours of delays and having not eaten since early that morning—could get him down.

Teresa took us to a little sandwich place right off the entrance to the interstate, and we all sat down and continued sharing stories and learning about one another. Fr. Agustino was a Franciscan Friar of the Renewal, living in the Bronx, though he was originally from San Antonio, Texas. The friars lived simply: slept on thin mats on the floor, ate simple meals in community, and spent tons of time in prayer each day. Their primary work was helping the poor, running home-less shelters and soup kitchens throughout inner-city New York, and evangelizing by witnessing to the joy of their radical life of poverty. Fr. Agustino loved being a friar—hearing him talk about his life was like watching a parent gush about how proud they are of their child. I was instantly captured by his personality and spirit. He traveled with less than a hundred dollars cash, just a few extra T-shirts for under his habit, and an old iPhone. He believed, firmly and intently, that the Lord would always provide. His faith and joy were incredible. We knew instantly: Fr. Agustino was the real deal.

The conversation continued long after we'd finished our meals. It was like none of us wanted to get up from the table. Sitting there, visiting and laughing and telling stories, was some of the most fun we'd ever had. Fr. Agustino had this unique ability to hang on our every word, as if it was the most precious thing ever said. He stared intently at us when we were talking, responding with his own thoughts only after he was certain we were finished. He asked thoughtful questions, offered his own insights, and told his own stories (each one better than the last). I could've sat there all afternoon listening to him, just soaking in his joy and holiness. I'd known him for less than an hour, but I felt as if I had known him my whole life.

We eventually got back on the road, ready to embroil ourselves in the traffic that would take us to campus and the conference that was starting that evening. After nearly twenty minutes of waiting to get back in the right lane to take the on-ramp onto the 405, Fr. Agustino declared with a chuckle, "This is why I just walk everywhere in New York!" It was fairly evident to all of us: this trip might take a while.

We inched along slowly, cars seeming to multiply around us as the on-ramp got closer and closer. Nearly forty-five minutes had knocked off only a couple miles of our journey, but fortunately our spirits were high and the conversation kept flowing. With the on-ramp only a few hundred feet ahead of us, we came to a dead stop under an overpass.

"Well, at least it's cooler," Fr. Agustino said with a smile as he reached over to turn the A/C fan down.

Grateful for my small town with only a few dozen streets and fairly light traffic, I stared mindlessly out the window, amazed that so many people could be crammed into such a tight space to get on just one interstate. Out of the corner of my eye, I saw some movement. As I looked over, I noticed a man sitting at the edge of the overpass, a cardboard sign propped up at his feet. "Family to feed" the sign read in black block letters. "No job. Please help." Scrawled underneath, in smaller print, "God bless you."

This was Los Angeles, I thought to myself. There are probably thousands of men just like him sitting underneath overpasses with identical signs. He wasn't really in the best location to solicit any money, either. An overpass, even if it's normally crammed with bumper-to-bumper traffic, isn't typically where people toss money into cups. With the windows rolled up, the radio blaring, and the A/C blasting, the last thing most Los Angeles folks would do right there is give money or food. Far too inconvenient. As I kept staring out the window at the guy, wondering why he chose to sit there and thinking about what his life must have been like up to that point, he stood up, grabbed his sign, and began walking across the lanes of traffic. Weaving in and out of each lane, I thought maybe he was going to start walking up to cars and knocking on the windows, asking for help. But his cardboard sign was hanging limply at his side. He seemed determined to get somewhere, his eyes fixed on something in the distance.

And then I realized: he was walking right toward us. With determination and speed, this guy was coming straight toward a little Mazda SUV with a youth minister, two teachers, and a Franciscan friar sitting inside trying to get to a youth conference. I reached over and instinctively hit the lock button on my door. No way this guy was getting into our car. We had somewhere to be, and a random bum under an overpass in Los Angeles traffic wasn't going to slow us down. I looked over at Tommy sitting next to me and pointed out the window at the guy. Tommy nodded his head and shrugged his shoulders, mouthing, "It'll be fine." Something in me was unsettled, though. It didn't feel quite right. This guy was headed right to our car. Out of the hundreds of other vehicles under that overpass and across six lanes of traffic, the scrawny homeless guy with the cardboard sign was making a beeline for us.

Teresa and Fr. Agustino seemed to be blissfully unaware of what I considered to be a full-on crisis about to take place. As they continued chatting in the front seat, I kept my eyes fixed on the man who was dodging in and out of vehicles that were slowly moving forward. When he was about thirty feet away from us, walking briskly to the front of our vehicle, staring right through the windshield, I again put my hand on the door, making sure the lock was engaged. Fr. Agustino rolled down his window.

"Hey, brother, what's your name?" Father said cheerfully as he extended his hand to the homeless man.

"My name is unimportant as I am a pilgrim seeking solace and comfort and help," the man blurted out at lightning speed, the words falling out of his mouth in a slur.

"A pilgrim, huh?" said Fr. Agustino, with a chuckle. "Well, so am I, man. So am I. Where are you headed?" And the two began talking. The homeless man spoke remarkably fast, his answers poetic and long-winded. He was a father who'd lost his job, a Christian man of faith who believed Jesus would take care of him, but Jesus was just letting him suffer for a little while to learn to trust him. He needed food for his family, though, so he was out under the overpass today hoping to meet an angel.

Fr. Agustino nodded his head the whole time the guy talked, eventually reaching out the window and taking the guy's hand into his own, staring deeply into his eyes. Traffic started to inch forward again, but Teresa kept her foot on the brake. Fr. Agustino was engaged in a full-fledged conversation with this man, and we clearly weren't going anywhere. We all looked at each other, a little confused as to what we should do. A few minutes passed, cars around us beginning to honk as they swerved out of our lane to go around us. Still, the two kept talking, oblivious to honking and the further delay they were causing.

"My brother, you are an amazing testament to faith," Fr. Agustino finally said, releasing the man's hand and reaching into the pocket of his habit. "Just a beautiful soul." He pulled out a twenty-dollar bill and held it out to the man, grabbed his hand again and said, "I want you to know I'm praying for you, okay? I want you to know how much you are loved, and I want you to know that I am so glad I met you today, brother."

The man's eyes began to well up with tears as he stared at Fr. Agustino and the twenty-dollar bill.

"No no, this is too much . . . it's too much," he began to stutter.

"It's not, brother. Take it. I have plenty," and Fr. Agustino pressed the twenty dollars into his hand. "I'm praying for you, friend." Fr. Agustino placed his hand on the man's forehead, signed the cross over him, gave him a blessing, and then said, "I love you, brother."

The man let go of Fr. Agustino's hand, raised his hands to the sky, and began shouting as loud as he could, "I have met a king among men today, brothers and sisters! I have met an angel who loves in such a beautiful way! I will not forget you, kind sir. I will not forget you, my friend. I will be praying for you, my brother!" He kept walking past our car, continuing to look up at the sky, hands clasped as he continued to shout, "Thank you! Thank you!"

Teresa started inching the car forward to reengage us in the long trek to the on-ramp. Fr. Agustino turned to us and said, "I'm sorry about that, y'all. Didn't mean to hold up traffic. But . . . I think we just met Jesus."

Tommy and I sat in stunned silence in the back seat, still in shock at what we'd just witnessed. A Franciscan friar from New York, sworn to live in poverty himself, traveling with less than a hundred bucks on his person, had taken 20 percent of all the money he had on him for the entire weekend and given it to a homeless man. Without hesitation or pause, he had visited with that man, listened to his story, and prayed over him with great confidence and comfort. I, on the other hand, had locked my door.

"I think I just saw you be Jesus" I replied, still stunned at the beauty of the moment.

"Isn't that what we're all supposed to do, Katie?" Fr. Agustino said, staring intently at me. "Be Jesus, and share the gift?"

FOUNDATION OF SERVICE

I was shocked when Fr. Agustino handed that homeless man a twenty-dollar bill. That's something I thought only rich folks do—passing out twenty dollars like it's no big deal. And yet Fr. Agustino, a man who sleeps on the floor, uses a cell phone only for traveling and ministry purposes, and spends his days with the inner-city poor of New York City, thought not of his own circumstances but generously gave to this man in need. He tangibly and visibly served that man by giving him money that he needed. He also provided for his spiritual needs by acknowledging him, loving him, and praying with him. Fr. Agustino was a servant in that moment—he served the man with his gift of money, and he served Jesus by imitating his generosity and compassion.

But how often do we think that's all service is—giving something material or doing something tangible? We "feed the hungry" by cooking meals in a soup kitchen. We "help the homeless" by volunteering at a shelter or donating old clothes. We "give to the needy" by throwing loose change in a cup or tossing a few dollars into the poor box at church or mowing the lawn of an elderly woman. We equate service with volunteering and think it's enough. We box ourselves in, thinking that the only (or best) way to serve Jesus is by doing something to help another with material needs

Doing physical tasks captures the external side of service. Handing someone twenty dollars or spending a week building a house with Habitat for Humanity is valuable and good and something we should all strive to do more of. But those physical acts are only a small portion of having a service-oriented attitude and heart. It is far more significant—in fact, it's far more powerful and important and necessary—for our service to first start with a desire, and attempt, to share Jesus with those whom we serve, because it is Jesus who should be the foundation, impetus, and inspiration of our desire to serve. Anyone can give twenty bucks to a homeless guy. Our goal—as people who have come to know, love, and follow Jesus—is to share him.

SHARING JESUS

We've been given a remarkable gift. Through our prayer, delving into the Bible, and participating in the sacramental life of the Church, we have met and been transformed by Jesus. That is not something we keep to ourselves. Meeting Jesus and falling in love with him sets the stage for me to go and share Jesus with others. Tangible acts of service—such as washing the dishes after dinner without being asked or going on that mission trip to an impoverished country—matter because we do them compelled by the love of Jesus. We serve not because we want a reward. We are called to serve and share what we have because Jesus has moved our hearts to give in the same way he has given: sacrificially, humbly, and with a desire to point to something greater than our own virtue or goodness—to point to the love of the Lord. We don't just do tasks set before us because it's the right thing to do. We serve—and do good works—because we can't help but strive to be like Jesus.

When Jesus washed the feet of the apostles at the Last Supper, he told them that he had come not to be served but to serve. Of all the people who most deserve to be served it's probably the very Son of God, right? He came to earth, preached, and healed for three years, and was about to be killed for doing so. If anyone deserved a little pampering and pomp and circumstance at his last meal with his best friends, it's Jesus! Instead, he wraps a towel around his waist, gets down on his hands and knees, and performs a menial task—washing mud and grime off the feet of simple men who wore sandals every day (and whose feet were probably gross). Jesus did the work of a slave. But his service—the tangible, material act—embodied a deeper message: his immense love for them. Jesus didn't just say nice things or pass out fancy presents to these men to show them he loved them: he did something that they would have thought beneath him. He did a servant's work, showing them just how valuable and precious they were. He was fully present to them, and bowed down to them in a simple act of love.

This is the Jesus we have met in prayer, scripture, and sacrament. That's the Jesus we are called to share with others—and we can do that with tangible acts of service that are inspired by a deep desire to love him and share that love. Our call to service is ultimately a call to imitate Jesus. Our lives should be a model of his life—the life we've come to know and been touched by as we have met him and grown to know and love him. Jesus ate with the sinners. He went to the colonies of lepers and spent time with them. He sat at the well and visited with the town whore. He was unafraid to be associated with the tax collectors. He hung out with the uneducated fishermen. He allowed himself to be betrayed and stretched his arms out upon a Cross and died, giving of himself in the most complete way possible: offering up his very life. This is our call to service. This is what it means to share the gift—sharing Jesus when we share our very selves, prompted and led by the relationship we have with him.

PERFECT SERVICE

If we want to perfectly serve the Lord in physical ways, we can't just think of it as checking off items on our Christian to-do list. We must first have hearts shaped by Jesus' love, which are humbly poured out in the tasks we do, whether menial and seemingly insignificant or grand and intense. Sharing Jesus first means that our words, actions, and deeds are aiding others and further transforming us, all at the same time. Thus our service is for others, but it is also us continuously pursuing a deeper encounter with and growth in love of Jesus. We witness to him when we do as he did, and we are called to give further witness by making it known that we have met him in prayer, related to him in scripture, and been transformed through the sacraments.

Jesus didn't just wash the feet of the apostles to ensure they didn't have smelly feet. He washed their feet to show them how much he loved them. He washed their feet and paved the path to the Cross, where he would do the ultimate act of service—lay down his life. When we are called to serve, we're meant to do the same: be fully present, show the infinite and perfect love of Jesus, and pave the way to give of ourselves completely by doing the task set before us—by serving in imitation of Jesus.

THE EFFECT

For over twenty years, the Diocese of Arlington, Virginia, has hosted an annual WorkCamp, bringing together about a thousand high school students and chaperones who commit themselves to a week of service work in the local community, serving the elderly, impoverished, and homebound. They rough it for the week—sleeping on the floor, showering in gym locker rooms, and eating basic and simple meals. Eight-hour work days are bookended with morning Mass and evening programs with faith-based talks, adoration, Confession, and opportunities for fellowship. There's no glamour to the WorkCamp experience. In fact, it's a tough week. The floors are hard, the showers are cold, the food isn't anything to write home about. Working in the hot sun building wheelchair ramps, repainting houses, cleaning out garages, and landscaping yards isn't easy. But every year, the Arlington Diocese maxes out the number of participants within weeks of opening up registration for the WorkCamp. It is easily one of their most popular programs, and teens come back year after year. They have no problem finding volunteers to serve as supervisors for the projects, they have a plethora of adults willing to chaperone and lead small groups, and tons of teens rush to get their spot secured.

In the summer of 2016, I had the chance to host and speak at each evening program at this WorkCamp. Within twenty-four hours of arriving on site and interacting with some of the teens and volunteers, something became evident: this week wasn't some isolated experience for anyone involved. People were profoundly transformed by WorkCamp, which is why they kept coming back year after year to work in the hot sun, sleep on the hard floor, take cold showers, and participate fully in this week of service. In fact, they were willing to pay upward of $500 to do it! Teens—high school students addicted to Snapchat who could add "professional Netflix binge watcher" to their resumes—were willing to pay to do service work. When I asked the director of the Office of Youth Ministry about this strange phenomenon (people willing to pay to do service), he looked at me, smiled, and said, "It's kind of cool, isn't it? We've learned that WorkCamp isn't something you do . . . WorkCamp is something done to you. You don't serve so much as let this experience serve you."

It clicked. So many people, summer after summer, had seen for themselves just what this weeklong service experience was all about, and they kept coming back because it wasn't just the isolated experience of building something or cleaning a room or painting a house. WorkCamp was a week designed for them to *do service work*, yes, but more importantly, it was meant to feed their souls, both through that very work and the numerous experiences to pray, grow in fellowship, and share their faith. Each morning at Mass and during every evening program, participants were challenged, inspired, and compelled to make their work a true work of the Lord. It wasn't just work for the sake of getting sweaty and having a wheelchair ramp to point to as "finished." It was work meant to help you experience sacrifice. It was service meant to put you in touch with those who show us the very face of Jesus—the people Jesus would have gone to himself—the poor, the sick, the helpless, and the unwanted. It was meant to work on your heart while also serving the greater needs of the community.

And shouldn't that be what all service truly is? If we're called to share the gift—responding to the movement of Jesus in our hearts because we have met him and grown to know and love him—then our service work begins and continues with him at the center.

On the final day of Arlington's annual WorkCamp, the people the campers have served all week are invited to share a meal and participate in a closing celebration. Those who have been served—and have served the participants by allowing them the chance to come work in their homes—gather to celebrate the good work that has been done all week. In 2016, about one-third of the residents served came to the closing program, and every one had a chance to share some thoughts about the week. An elderly World War II veteran named Sam stood up and, with tears in his eyes, poured his heart out about how if everyone in the world was as kind as the young people who had worked on his roof that week, then the world would be a much better place. A woman with a handicapped daughter shared that all week, the work crew assigned to her house had taken shifts going inside to sit with her wheelchair-bound, mute daughter and visit with her, sharing stories, playing board games, and praying with her. She couldn't believe that not only had they gotten a wheelchair ramp, but they'd also gained new friends and her daughter hadn't stopped smiling all week. These moments of praise and gratitude continued for nearly an hour as resident after resident shared how they'd been so touched by the hard work, kindness, and Christian faith they'd seen from the work crews that had served in their homes.

As the sharing began to wrap up, a Muslim woman in the traditional Islamic dress stood up and took the microphone. A hush fell over the entire crowd as she softly began speaking.

"As you can tell, I am a Muslim woman. And you are all Christian."

The silence in the room was deafening. Three days before, we had all offered up special intentions at Mass for the victims of a radical Islamic terrorist-inspired shooting in the airport in Istanbul, Turkey.

"I know that it may seem that my religion and your religion are not always . . . compatible." There was a long pause as she looked out over the crowd.

"But you Christians still came into my home . . . and you served us. This week I had three work crews at my house painting the outside and redoing the roof. You worked tirelessly, and my home is now more beautiful and safe. I started this week with four children. I am ending it with twenty-four."

The entire room erupted into applause, amazed at the joy, gratitude, and simple beauty of this woman. As the applause died down, she very quietly said, "I am not a Christian. I don't know your Jesus very well. But I believe I have met him this week . . . in each of you."

HANDS AND FEET

When we think of service, we need to open our minds and recognize that it is first and foremost about sharing Jesus by being Jesus to others. We are called to share the gift we've been given through our encounter with him by doing what he did: giving of ourselves, sacrificially, to others. Sometimes this includes tangible works of service—the mission trip, the Habitat for Humanity build, or the yard work. Sometimes it involves simply being with other people, listening and sharing—a true ministry of presence, serving them by sharing time and space with them. And sometimes it involves giving testimony and witness to your faith in and relationship with Jesus, even when it's challenging, scary, or could cause you discomfort.

Service in your Home

Very practically, if you want to share the gift of Jesus with others, it probably starts in simple ways—and right in your own home. Service doesn't always mean going to a third world country and serving the poorest of the poor. Serving the people you're around day by day, such as your parents and siblings, is the most straightforward way to begin sharing the gift of your encounter with Jesus and living sacrificially like he did. These small acts of service can often be the prompt and inspiration to want to serve more, and have the attitude of one who lives for others and wants to share Jesus rather than selfishly gaining popularity or fortune.

Doing simple household chores, which are usually tedious and menial (and that very few people enjoy doing) are small ways to show the love of Jesus that has compelled you to have a servant's heart and give as he gave. The tangible household tasks listed below can also be turned into opportunities to spend time in prayer. If you're doing the job alone, maybe pray the Rosary or think further about the daily gospel you read. If it's in the evening, go through your nightly examination of conscience and make your mental checklist of how you can improve for the next day. If you're working with a sibling or parent, take the time to visit with them and share what's on your heart and mind. This just may lead to fruitful conversation and a chance to further connect with someone you love but may not have spent much time with lately. Consider how the following tasks can serve your family:

• Wash the dishes.

- Make all the beds in the house.
- Vacuum the living room.
- Do your family's laundry, and fold and hang it for them.
- Give up the remote control and let someone else choose what to watch.
- Take your family out for dessert.
- Help with the yard work—mow the lawn, use the trimmer, or sweep the porch or walkway.
- Clean and organize the garage, attic, or cluttered storage spaces.
- Cook your family a meal (and then eat it together, without phones or the television on) or help your parents as they prepare a meal.
- Help your siblings with their homework.
- Babysit your siblings (for free).

There are countless ways to do practical tasks in your home to show how much you care about your family and how much you want to have a service-oriented heart and mind. Pay attention to what's going on in your home and you'll probably notice where help is needed and ways that you can contribute more fully, especially without being asked or told to do something. It's when we serve willingly, because we want to share and be like Jesus, that we are truly sharing the gift that has been given to us.

Service in your Church

Becoming more involved in the life of your parish and youth ministry program or group can give you the chance to serve within the Church itself. Serving simply in your home helps you strengthen your "service muscle." Finding opportunities to serve with others, or from your strengths, can give you further inspiration to do the good work of being like and sharing Jesus. Get started with the following ideas:

- Sign up to become a lector, proclaiming the readings at Mass (both weekdays and on Sunday).

- If you're confirmed, serve as an Extraordinary Minister of Holy Communion.
- Volunteer as an altar server.
- Offer your talents to the parish:
    → Are you tech savvy? Volunteer to help build (or improve) the parish website or bulletin.
    → Can you sing? Join the choir.
    → Are you a good listener or people person? Find some home-bound parishioners and offer to visit them, bringing a meal or taking them Holy Communion once a week.
    → Can you build things and do good grunt work? Find out who needs yard work or housework done and offer to help complete these tasks.
    → Do you like kids? Sign up to staff the parish's Vacation Bible School, serve at children's church, or provide babysitting at parish events.
    → Do you have an eye for design? Sign up to work with the committee that decorates the church for various liturgical seasons and celebrations.
    → Can you cook or bake? Offer to cook meals for families in need or provide food for parish events, such as fundraisers or parish picnics.
- Sign up for the yearly workcamp or mission trip.
    → There are many service-oriented programs offered, usually during the summer, whether through your individual parish, diocese, or an independent organization. Some include Catholic Heart Workcamp, SHINE Work Camp, Fully Alive! WorkCamp (and many more).

Service in your Community

We don't live in a vacuum, isolated unto ourselves. We live in community. We are surrounded by others, and it only takes a little self-awareness to realize how much we can do for other people in our homes and parishes. At the same time, we must also look to the larger community—the city where we live, the country in which we dwell, the world we call home. One single person can effect great change by living with a servant's heart and committing themselves to aiding others in both big and small ways. Find an organization or get involved with a larger project in your area that gives your service wider reach. Even if you are doing something small and simple within that larger work, you can serve your community in a very real way. Consider helping with the following efforts:

- Catholic Relief Services Project Rice Bowl
  - → Each year, CRS provides small, cardboard bowls that you can place your spare change into each day for a set period of time (usually around Lent and Advent). The money you collect then goes to provide food to people in impoverished countries. As little as three and four dollars can provide meals for a family for an entire week. What we consider loose change can literally be a means of survival for those living in poverty.

- Habitat for Humanity
  - → This nonprofit is built around the idea that providing housing, and practical job training for those who are given these homes, can help rebuild the community. You can sign up to work for a Habitat for Humanity build in your area and do everything from pouring foundation to floating sheetrock and painting walls. There's something very satisfying about working with your hands to build something tangible, and working with others in your community can show you the bigger picture of your service's impact.

- Homebound or Nursing Home Residents
  - → There are thousands of elderly and sick people living in nursing homes, unvisited and lonely. Call a nursing home facility and offer to play bingo with the residents or ask them to give you a list of which residents haven't been visited by anyone in a long time. Go spend a few hours with them, listening to their stories and developing relationships with them.

- Fundraising for Local Charities
  - → Many worthy causes are advertised all day, every day. Find one that you're passionate about and put in time and effort to promote the cause and get people to charitably donate to the cause. Maybe it's a fundraiser to provide care for someone battling a disease or to rebuild a home lost in a natural disaster. Maybe it's a fundraiser to aid an organization in continuing their charitable work. It could be a fundraiser to help a down-on-their-luck family buy groceries or pay the bills. Find something that speaks to your heart.

- Care Bags for Homeless Residents
  - → Whether you live in a big city or a small town, there are probably people around you who don't have proper shelter, clothing, or confidence in where they will find their next meal. A simple way to help those folks is by making "care bags" and keeping them in your car, giving them to those in need when you see them. Fill up a gallon-sized ziplock bag (or a small, reusuable plastic container) with weather-appropriate items such as socks, gloves, a hat or scarf, hand sanitizer, toothbrush and toothpaste, water bottle, granola bars or small snacks, a gift card to a fast-food place, and directions to a local soup kitchen or homeless shelter.

SMALL THINGS. GREAT LOVE.

It would be nearly impossible to provide an exhaustive list of "how and where you can serve." That's a book unto itself. But in reality, you don't need that. All you need is a love of Jesus and a desire to give of yourself, and you will begin to see the numerous possibilities to live and act as a servant to others, in his name. It's your love of Jesus and his love of you—and your knowledge of who he is—that will compel you to give of yourself as a servant. It's why Fr. Agustino stopped traffic. It's why hundreds of people go to the Arlington WorkCamp each summer. It's why mission trips are one of the most popular activities for parishes and youth ministry programs in the country. People are driven by a desire to share the great gift that has been given to them—and starting small, offering your talents, and looking to give back to the larger community will allow you to fully realize and share the love of Jesus that fills your heart.

Just look at St. Teresa of Calcutta. A simple woman, less than five feet tall, she was able to start one of the most profoundly beautiful and passionate religious orders that humbly and charitably serves the poorest of the poor and sickest of the sick. And she did it by simply being present to people, working to give them dignity in their dying moments and providing for their most basic needs. It all began because she was compelled by a love of Jesus to love those in need. While sitting on a train heading to her annual retreat, she felt the tug on her heart and heard the voice of the Lord to do something radical for him—to go to those in need, live among them, and serve them with a willing heart, to hold their hands, to talk with them. Her call was to love the poor and sick, even though they offered nothing materially valuable or tangibly productive to society. A desire to share the gift of Jesus, and to live as he lived and do as he does, has inspired countless others of his followers to do the same—to serve in small ways with a great love, both of the other and of Jesus himself.

When we share the gift and become servants to others, in both big and small ways, we are ultimately responding to the transformation that has taken place within our hearts because we have met and come to know Jesus.

AFTERWORD

Some families take vacations to the beach, lounging in the soft sand as the sun beats down upon them. Some families go to Disney World, standing in long lines to ride thrilling rides and eat Mickey Mouse-shaped popsicles. But my family went to Disney World and realized we weren't really roller-coaster people. And since we're all fair-skinned, the beach was always a death trap, so we certainly didn't want to go there. For years, my mom, dad, sister, and I would travel up to Gatlinburg, Tennessee, for ten days every summer and go hiking in the Great Smoky Mountains. We were that family . . . the one that wakes up at 5:00 a.m., loads up backpacks with protein bars and water bottles, and blazes trails through the woods to find a beautiful waterfall or hopefully spot a (somewhat friendly) bear.

As a little kid, I loved these vacations. We'd rent a cabin in the woods, Mom and Dad would let us stay up later than normal watching movies, and we would get to see actual hills and mountains (which are nonexistent in very flat, below-sea-level Louisiana). But as I got older and hit those angst-filled teenage years, I began to dread family vacation to Tennessee. I didn't want to wake up at 5:00 a.m. to hike. Isn't vacation supposed to be relaxing? Aren't we supposed to rest and recover from the daily grind? What could possibly be fun about carrying snacks up a mountain to see water flowing off a cliff? We can easily find a picture of that on the Internet and stay in the comfort of a nice, air-conditioned hotel room with HBO and room service.

So I did what any typical teenager would do . . . I complained loudly, offered my own solutions and ideas for what I considered to be these "problem vacations," and grumbled the whole time. But my parents were insistent: This is what we Prejeans did for our family vacation. We went to Tennessee. We stayed in a cabin. We hiked mountains.

The summer before my sophomore year of high school, we loaded up Dad's Excursion and set out for our annual trip to my least favorite place in America for the worst ten days of my year. Fifteen hours in the truck later, we got to our cabin and began unloading our supplies. As I pulled suitcases out of the back, I saw a pamphlet crumbled up in the corner of a box. Across the top, in bold font, it read: "Mount LeConte: breathtaking views at 6,500 feet." I grabbed the pamphlet, brought it inside, and found my dad.

"So are we doing a new trail this year?" I asked, my words dripping with sarcasm as I held out the brochure.

Dad smoothed out the pamphlet in his hands and started chuckling as he saw what it was. "Oh, yeah! I grabbed this last year from the visitor's center. It's a pretty strenuous hike past Caveman's Bluff. I doubt we can handle doing it. It's supposed to be fairly steep."

Arrogantly, I scoffed. "Well, we're here . . . might as well try to do something different and not just repeat the same trails over and over again."

My dad stared me down and sharply said, "Well, you know what then? Fine. We'll do this hike. And it'll probably hurt and we'll be exhausted. But if you're going to complain the whole time we're here, then hiking eight miles straight up a mountain might be enough to shut you up." He stormed off, leaving me standing there with my suitcase by my feet, the pamphlet wrinkled on the cabin's kitchen counter.

The days ticked by slowly, each one seemingly longer than the last. The vacation was just like every other one before . . . we'd wake up, go hiking, come home and eat hotdogs or hamburgers, and then go roam around Gatlinburg, visiting little shops, playing putt-putt, and taking scenic photos of the panoramic mountain views. Dad hadn't brought up the Mount LeConte hike since we'd discussed it when we first arrived, but we also hadn't yet hiked Caveman's Bluff, the first part of the trail that would lead to that longer hike. By day six, I'd assumed he'd forgotten about it, until at dinner that evening he pulled the pamphlet out of his pocket.

"So, y'all, I have an idea. Why don't we do this hike tomorrow? It's longer than what we're used to, sixteen miles round-trip, but the views are awesome."

My mom and sister were instantly on board, excited about a new challenge. I remained silent, staring down at my food. Sure, I'd brought it up with my dad first, but I really didn't want to hike sixteen miles and be exhausted and sore.

"Katie?" Dad said. "What do you think? This was your big idea, wasn't it? To do something different on vacation for a change? Well, here's a different hike!" He started laughing, and I grumblingly agreed. No use fighting a battle I wasn't going to win.

The next morning, we woke up at our usual 5:00 a.m., loaded the supplies, and set off for the trailhead of Mount LeConte. It began as most of our hikes usually did: the four of us walking in single file on a narrow trail, my dad leading us and my mom bringing up the rear, Laura and I in the middle. I kept my head down and walked briskly. I may be there, hiking the stupid long trail I'd mentioned but I didn't have to enjoy any of this. Two and a half miles in, we reached Caveman's Bluff, a large open-faced cave on the side of the mountain, covered in red sand and large boulders. We stopped for a brief break, knowing we still had five and a half miles to go up to Mount LeConte's peak.

Ten minutes passed, protein bars were passed around, and then Dad shouted, "All right! Let's do this!" and he set off for the narrow path past the open cave that would lead us another few miles up the mountain. "Hey, Katie!" he yelled, "Do you want to take the lead?"

"I'll just slow us down," I grumbled.

"That's fine! We probably should slow down anyway! We aren't enjoying this!"

"Fine," I muttered, squeezing past him, beginning the ascent up a stupid mountain I didn't want to climb.

We continued hiking in relative silence, my dad making an occasional joke or my sister asking for a quick break. As we got farther along the trail, the air became thinner and the path more narrow, rocks jutting out from the sides, causing us to lose our footing and trip from time to time. I kept plugging along, head down, feet moving quickly. The sooner we get to the top, I thought, the sooner this nonsense will be over and I can be back at the cabin, locked in my bedroom, surfing the channels, and finding something to watch on TV. All I wanted to do was get to the top, because the top of the mountain was the entire reason we were hiking this trail in the first place. The views were supposed to be spectacular, so let's hurry up and get there.

After an hour, my dad yelled out, "Katie! Slow down! Katie! Come back!" I stopped, looked behind me, and realized my family wasn't behind me anymore. I turned around and began walking down the trail, rounding the corner and seeing the three of them standing on an overhang, looking out at a spectacular view. I'd walked right past a beautiful overlook over the Smokey Mountains. This brief break in the trees gave way to a gorgeous view, sunlight bursting across the mountains, casting shadows across the range.

"I didn't even notice this," I said as I walked up to them, panting heavily as I caught my breath.

"You were practically running," my sister said.

"And your head was down," my mom said.

"Oh. Sorry, I just want to get to the top." I mumbled as I stood there, looking out at the mountains, shocked that I hadn't noticed the overhang just a few moments before when I'd passed.

"Katie, you've gotta slow down or you're gonna miss this stuff," my dad said, walking over to me and placing his hand on my shoulder. "It's the journey, not the destination, that we're here for."

I rolled my eyes as I said, "Way to be super cheesy, Dad."

"Oh, I know it's cheesy. But it's true. Just look . . ." and he pointed out at the beautiful view. "The journey gave us this view."

We finished the hike an hour or so later, making it to the top of Mount LeConte just in time for lunch. The view from the top was gorgeous—a stunning look over the Great Smoky Mountains from more than 6,500 feet. The thin air was cool, the breeze hitting us as we sat on rocking chairs set out across the mountain lodge's front porch. People staying at the lodge overnight were milling around, cracking jokes, and swapping hiking stories. We sat there, eating our food and looking out over the view, each one of us hoping that we'd get some peace and quiet to enjoy what was easily one of the best and most beautiful things we'd ever seen. These people were being loud and boisterous and ruining what we thought was going to be a quiet, mountaintop moment.

As if on cue, we all looked at each other, nodded in agreement, threw away our lunch trash, and began hiking back down to the overhang on the trail that we'd found. As we arrived at the break in the trees and stopped to look out on the view we'd seen earlier, my dad looked over at me, a smile on his face. "See, the journey was worth it, wasn't it? Because we found this and now we're back, and it's even better than our destination."

My mom passed out candy bars she'd bought at the lodge on top of the mountain. I took a bite out of my Snickers bar, and with a full mouth, loudly proclaimed, "Yes, Dad . . . you're right. It's the journey, not the destination." I rolled my eyes as I playfully punched his arm.

"Mark this moment down!" my dad shouted. "Katie admitted I was right! Put that in writing, because she'll never admit it again!" We all started laughing as we kept staring out over the spectacular view halfway up the trailhead to Mount LeConte. The journey had given us a better view than what we'd been looking for, just as Dad had said. The journey, not the intended destination, was the best experience we could've had—for it was on that journey that we discovered something beautiful, life-changing, and worth experiencing.

Meeting Jesus and getting to know him is a lot like climbing a mountain. We set out on a journey with an intended destination: knowing Jesus as best we can. But if all we do is keep our eyes fixed on the end product and assume that we'll achieve our goal when we get there, then we won't notice what's happening along the away. We won't appreciate what's happening within our hearts and minds as we learn to pray, our words simple and our hearts perhaps a little closed. We'll fail to notice how childlike and open-minded we may be when we open a gospel and read a story with fresh eyes. We might forget how powerful and precious the Eucharist actually is or how great a gift we've been given in the chance to regularly go to Confession. We might rush past chances to serve and be the hands and feet of Jesus, sharing his love as it fuels our every thought and action.

Our journey to follow Jesus is less a hike up a mountain that we stand atop, with arms triumphantly raised, shouting, "I did it! I met Jesus!" Our journey is *with* Jesus, an adventure we set out on with him by our side, each step of the way a beautiful victory and destination in and of itself. We don't ever complete this journey. The adventure never ends, because we always have the chance to stop at different overhangs and look out at a spectacular view. New things will be manifested to us, the journey becoming longer, more beautiful, and more fruitful with every step. We don't just pray a set amount of time, check it off our to-do list, and call it done. We don't read the Bible from cover to cover and proclaim that we have learned the Word in its entirety. We don't go to Mass once and believe we've obtained all the Eucharist has to offer. We don't serve for a set number of minutes each day so we can meet our "charitable quota" for the afternoon. We set out on a journey intended to get us to Jesus . . . and as we take off on this adventure, every step of the way becomes a gift and beautiful experience that draws us closer and closer to who he is.

He's the one with you on the journey—your companion on this adventure we call life. He's the one who loves you beyond compare and wants to be with you at every twist and turn. Jesus is the Word made Flesh, dwelling among us, residing within us, drawing us ever closer to relationship with him. How can you get to know him? Journey with him in prayer, lifting up your broken, confused, muddled heart and sharing the very depths of your soul with his pure and perfect heart. How can you get to know him? Journey with him through the Bible, taking in the Word to get to know the Word, seeing his life and recognizing that he is not a distant character in some ancient tale, but someone who knows and relates to what you experience. How can you get to know Jesus, truly? Journey with him in the grace of the sacrament, receiving his very Body and Blood and being washed in his abundant mercy, forever changed by this most intimate and perfect encounter with him. How can you get to know this one who loves you perfectly and desires to be with you? Journey with him as you seek to give, serve, and respond to the needs of others, compelled by the encounter you have had with him.

A young man in Los Angeles asked me questions that, at their root, can only be answered in part. The process of answering these questions is never complete because the adventure to and with Jesus is never finished. It is a *lifelong* adventure to follow Jesus, a journey that is far more valuable than its destination, because when you've reached the destination (eternal union with Jesus in heaven), you will realize that following him was pursuing and living heaven all along. You discover Jesus and are transformed by your relationship with Jesus by seeing that he is your companion on the journey, not just a prize to be won at the end. You follow Jesus when you realize he is walking with you on this lifelong adventure . . . and nothing is better, more exciting, more fulfilling, or more necessary.

So get started. See you on the trail.

ACKNOWLEDGMENTS

This book was a labor of love, far more difficult to write than *Room 24* and, I imagine, more challenging than any other book that will someday come. It wouldn't exist without the persistent and patient encouragement of one of the finest editors in the business, Eileen Ponder, who has become a person I can't imagine my life without. Her steady hand and guidance, along with the diligent work of all the fine folks at Ave Maria Press, are the only reasons I'm ever able to write anything of value. I'm grateful for the time they gave me to answer that young man's questions.

This book was a response to two questions from a young man whose name I do not know. Should he ever find and read this book, I hope it satisfies that insatiable thirst he had for Jesus and helps him meet the one who loves him best and knows him fully. If he makes it to the end and sees this, then I hope he knows how much I owe him: without those questions, I don't think my faith would be where it is today.

A young woman I met at a conference and struck up a friendship with read every version of this book, giving me advice and insight into what exactly teenagers would want to read and need to know. Margaret, you're a treasure and I'm so happy to know you.

I wouldn't know Jesus, nor would I have the impetus to continue growing in my relationship with him, were it not for my mom and dad. Their faith and witness to daily encounters with him have been the best model and inspiration in my life. Thank you for the gift of my life and for giving me faith. I grew up with those parents with only one other person, my sister, Laura. Her genius, wit, wisdom, humor, and beautiful faith constantly amaze me. God gave me a sister who keeps me on my toes, pushes me to be better, and draws me back to Jesus every chance she gets. Thank you for being my best friend.

I'm blessed to be on the journey with Jesus, walking hand in hand with the love of my life, my Tommy. Every time I sat down to write, he was there with a cup of coffee, an encouraging word, an editing eye, or a silly joke to make me laugh. And even when I'm not writing, he is there, reminding me again and again how much he loves me. I don't say and show it enough, because I'm not the romantic he is . . . but Tommy, my life would not be what it is without you and I love you more than life itself.

And lastly, to the person who was literally with me at every moment of writing this book, my little Rosie: your journey with Jesus and your adventures are just beginning. It is the greatest honor of my life to be your mom, and I hope I can take you to the Lord every chance I get. Thanks for waiting to be born until the manuscript was turned in, kiddo. I can't wait to see where this life, and Jesus, take you.

Katie Prejean McGrady is a Catholic speaker and the author of *Room 24*. She shares the Gospel with a unique blend of humor and storytelling that weaves in theological truths to engage audiences of all ages and sizes. She has spoken at the National Catholic Youth Conference, Steubenville Youth Conferences, the National Conference for Catholic Youth Ministry, the National Catholic Educational Conference, the Los Angeles Religious Education Congress, and in dioceses and parishes across North America. Prejean McGrady has appeared on EWTN, CatholicTV, Relevant Radio, Radio Maria, and on SiriusXM's The Catholic Channel.

She loves to read, dances terribly, frequently laughs at the numerous awkward situations she encounters, and watches NBA and college basketball obsessively. Prejean McGrady has her bachelor's degree in theology from the University of Dallas and is working on her master's degree from the Augustine Institute. She lives with her husband, Tommy, daughter, Rosie, and dog, Barney, in Lake Charles, Louisiana.

Also by Katie Prejean McGrady

Five years after she graduated from high school, teacher, youth minister, and sought-after speaker Katie Prejean McGrady returned to her alma mater in Lake Charles, Louisiana, to teach freshman theology. In the early years of her career, McGrady's hormonal, sometimes grumpy, and often confused students taught her what it means to evangelize. Her frequently witty and always candid stories—and the ten lessons she offers—will inspire anyone who works with youth in the Church today.

"Brimming with inspirational vision and practical advice."
Chris Stefanick
Founder and President of *Real Life Catholic*

AVE
Ave Maria Press

Look for this title wherever books and e-books are sold.
For more information, visit avemariapress.com.